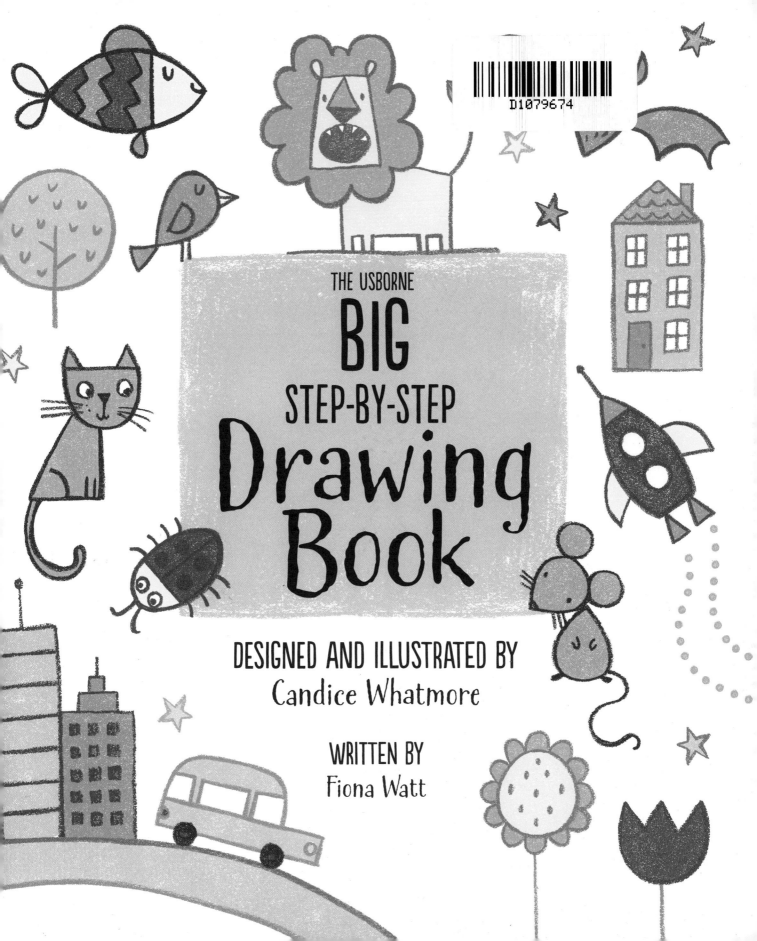

THE USBORNE

BIG

STEP-BY-STEP

Drawing Book

DESIGNED AND ILLUSTRATED BY
Candice Whatmore

WRITTEN BY
Fiona Watt

How to draw a rocket

Your turn...

① Draw a long thin rectangle...

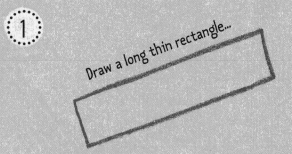

② a triangle at each end...

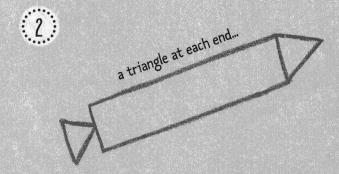

③ tail fins... windows...

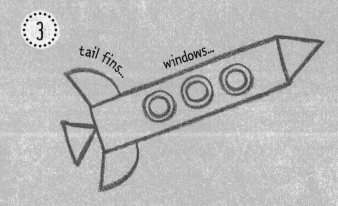

④ flames... and stripes.

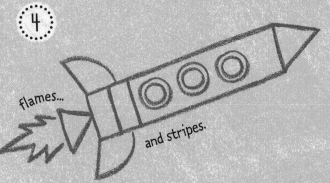

You could vary the
shape of a rocket.

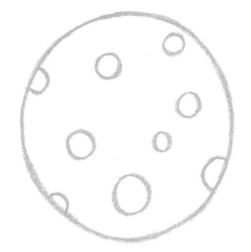

How to draw a flower...

① Draw a circle...

② lots of petals...

③ lots of dots... a stalk...

④ and two leaves.

Your turn...

and another.

1   Draw a 'U' shape...

2   a zigzag line...

3   a stalk...

4   and two leaves.

Add some flowers to these stalks...

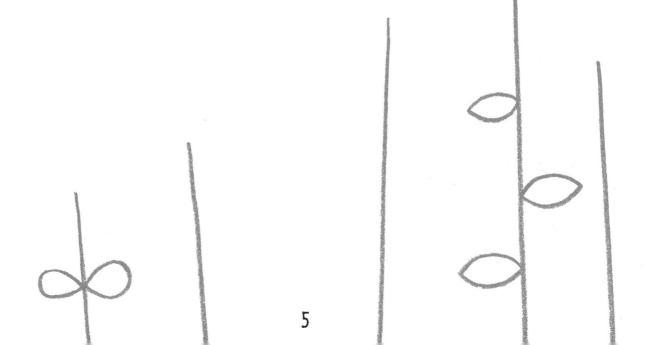

5

How to draw a fish

Your turn...

1

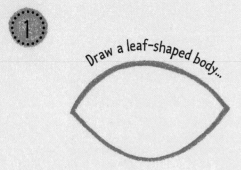

Draw a leaf-shaped body...

2

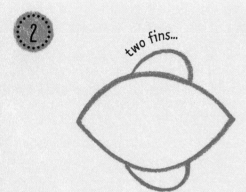

two fins...

3

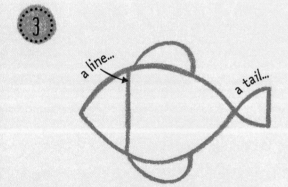

a line...

a tail...

4

and an eye and mouth.

Add spots to the body, if you like.

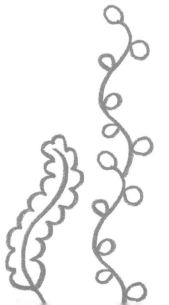

Try this... you can create lots of different fish by using stripes, zigzags, spots or dots to decorate. You can also try the following...

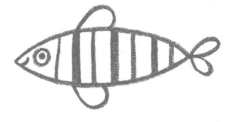

different-shaped fins   a smaller body   or a longer body

How to draw a zebra

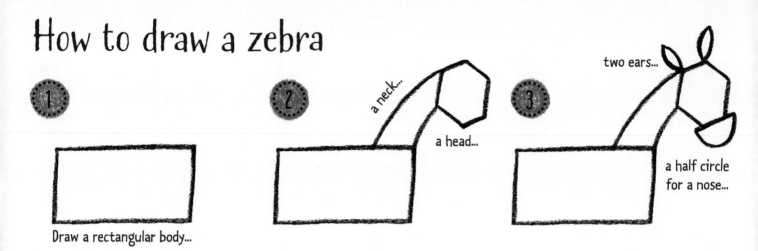

1

Draw a rectangular body...

2

a neck...

a head...

3

two ears...

a half circle for a nose...

Your turn...

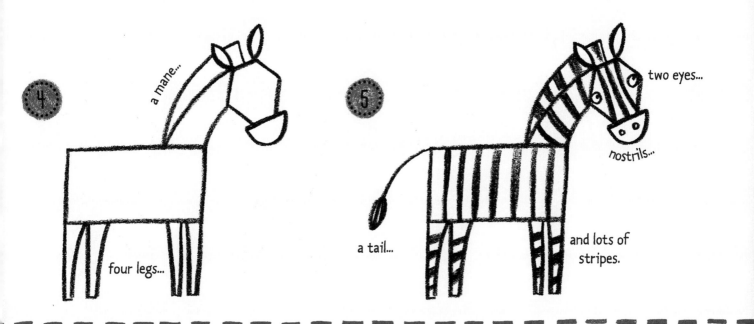

4 a mane... four legs...

5 two eyes... nostrils... a tail... and lots of stripes.

How to draw a superhero

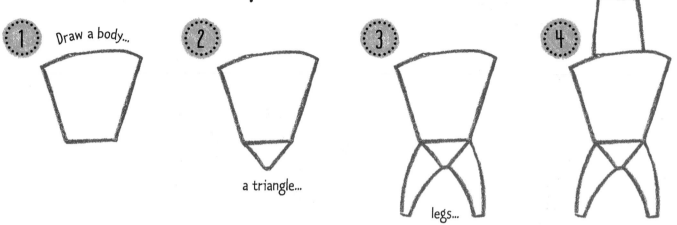

1 Draw a body...

2 a triangle...

3 legs...

4 a head...

Your turn...

5 a face mask...

two arms...

6 a neck...

gloves...

feet...

7 hair...

eyes, ears, a nose and a mouth...

and a cape.

Try this...

To make a superhero fly, draw the body and head as before, then...

draw one arm up like this...

a logo...

legs like this...

and a cape.

How to draw a raccoon

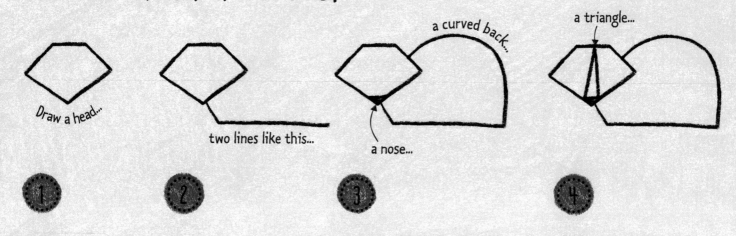

Draw a head...

two lines like this...

a nose...

a curved back...

a triangle...

① ② ③ ④

Your turn...

12

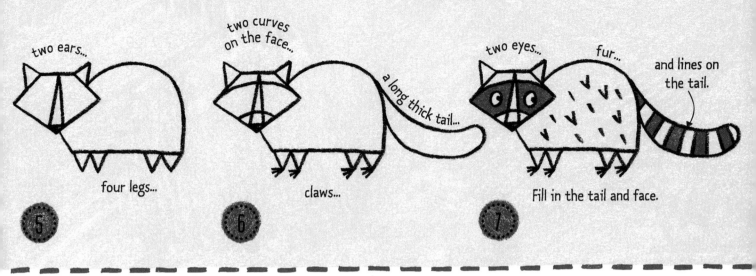

two ears...

four legs...

two curves on the face...

claws...

a long thick tail...

two eyes...

fur...

and lines on the tail.

Fill in the tail and face.

5

6

7

How to draw a robot

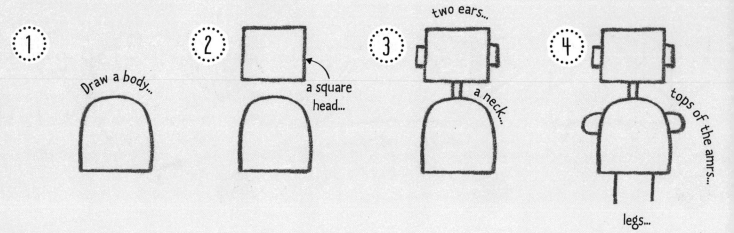

1 Draw a body...

2 a square head...

3 two ears... a neck...

4 tops of the amrs... legs...

Your turn...

(5) a face panel...

arms and hands...

feet...

(6) eyes and a mouth...

a tummy and buttons...

(7) and an antenna.

Fill in the face panel.

Try this...

Draw different shaped bodies for your robot. You could use wheels instead of legs too. Here are some ideas. You could copy these or invent your own.

How to draw a toucan

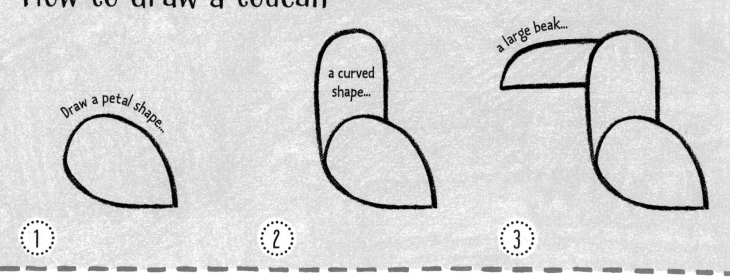

Draw a petal shape...

a curved shape...

a large beak...

① ② ③

Your turn...

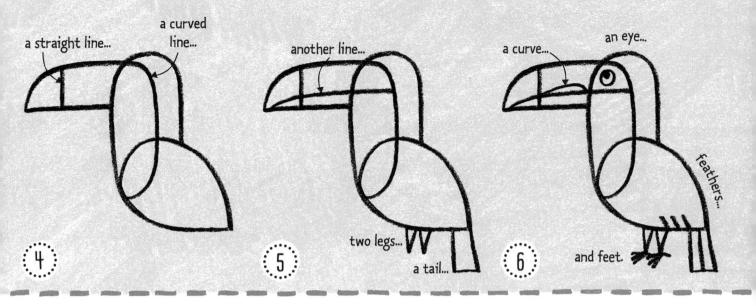

a straight line...

a curved line...

④

another line...

two legs...

a tail...

⑤

a curve...

an eye...

feathers...

and feet.

⑥

Try this...

Once you have drawn your toucan, you could use red, green, blue, yellow and black pens or pencils to fill it in like this.

How to draw trees

Your turn...

1 Draw a teardrop shape...

2 and a trunk and branches.

1 A circle...

2 and a trunk and branches.

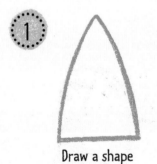

1 Draw a shape like this...

2 and a trunk and branches.

1 A cloud shape...

2 and a trunk and branches.

18

Try adding leaves...

or fruit.

How to draw a cat

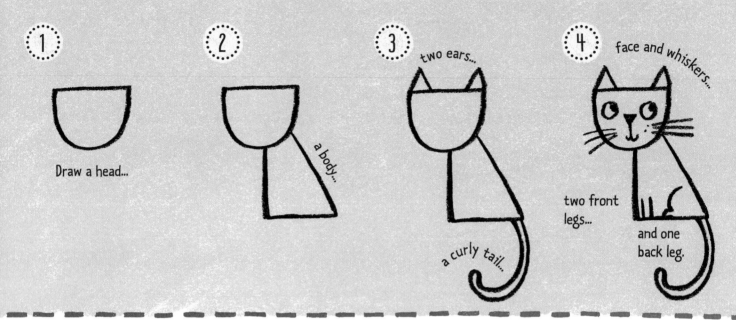

1 Draw a head...

2 a body...

3 two ears... a curly tail...

4 face and whiskers... two front legs... and one back leg.

Your turn...

How to draw a fairy

① Draw a circle...

② a triangular body... a line...

③ two curved lines... another curve...

④ long hair... two arms... two legs...

Your turn...

5 strands of hair... hands... feet...

6 eyes, a nose, a mouth and ears... wings... frills...

7 magical stars... and a wand.

How to draw a jellyfish

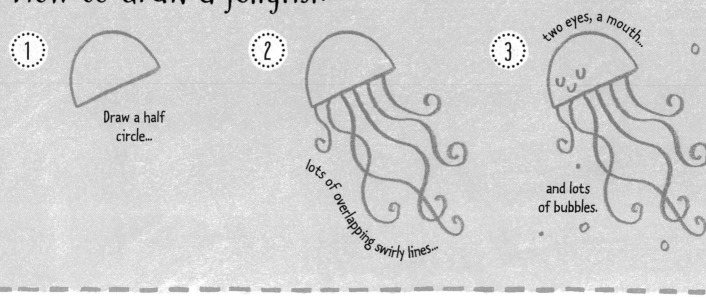

1 Draw a half circle...

2 lots of overlapping swirly lines...

3 two eyes, a mouth... and lots of bubbles.

Your turn...

How to draw a wizard

Your turn...

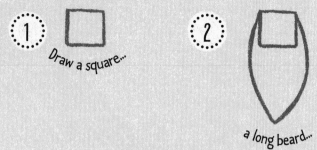

① Draw a square...

② a long beard...

③ a pointed hat...

a body...

④ two sleeves...

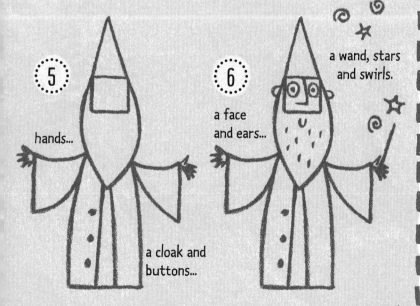

⑤ hands...

a cloak and buttons...

⑥ a face and ears...

a wand, stars and swirls.

How to draw a house

Your turn...

1 Draw a rectangle...

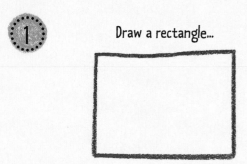

2 a rectangular roof...

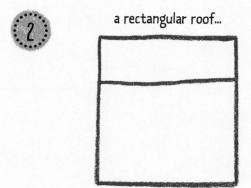

3 a triangle...

windows and a door...

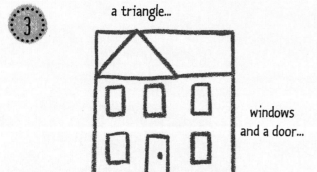

4 roof tiles...

lines on the windows...

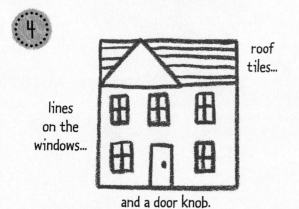

and a door knob.

Try this... create different houses by just changing a few things. How about...

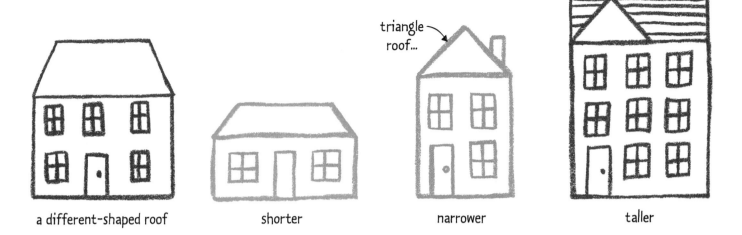

a different-shaped roof   shorter   narrower   taller

triangle roof...

How to draw a builder

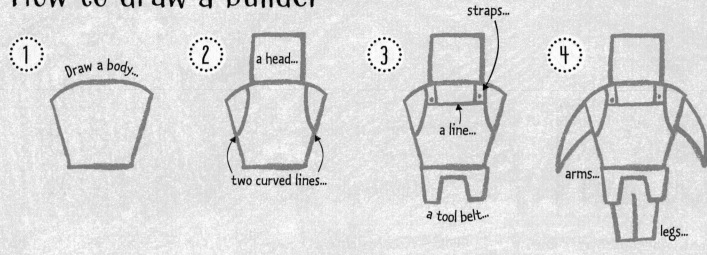

1 Draw a body...

2 a head...
two curved lines...

3 straps...
a line...
a tool belt...

4 arms...
legs...

Your turn...

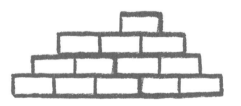

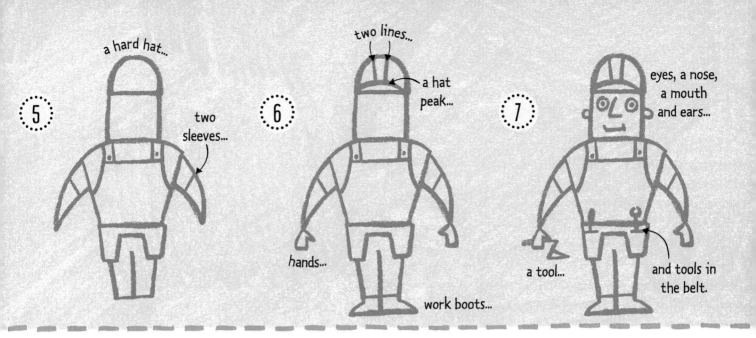

5 · a hard hat...

two sleeves...

6 · two lines...

a hat peak...

hands...

work boots...

7 · eyes, a nose, a mouth and ears...

a tool...

and tools in the belt.

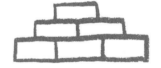

How to draw a meerkat

Your turn...

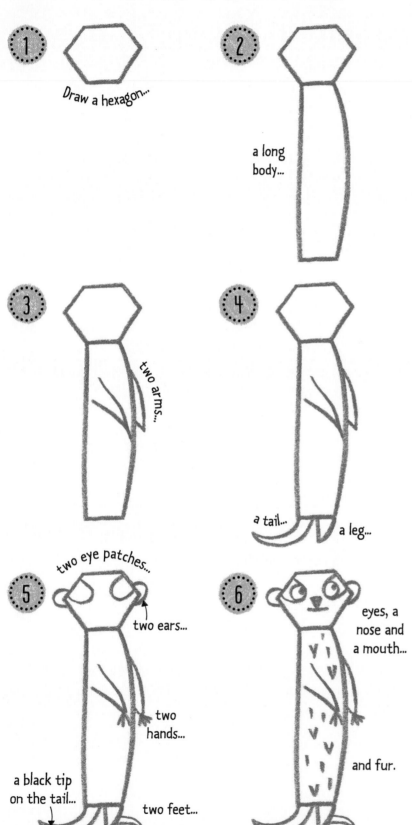

1 Draw a hexagon...

2 a long body...

3 two arms...

4 a tail... a leg...

5 two eye patches... two ears... two hands... a black tip on the tail... two feet...

6 eyes, a nose and a mouth... and fur.

How to draw a panda

1. Draw a head...

2. a round body...

3. and four legs.

Your turn...

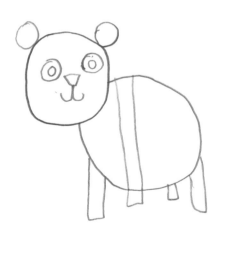

Add two ears...

panda eyes...

4

two lines
across the body...

5

and a nose and mouth.

6

Use black to fill in the shapes.

Try this...

For a panda standing up, either copy this one or follow the steps for the bear on the next page, but don't add the long nose when you get to step 5. Instead...

fill in the ears...

add a
panda face...

fill the
front legs...

then the back legs.

How to draw a bear

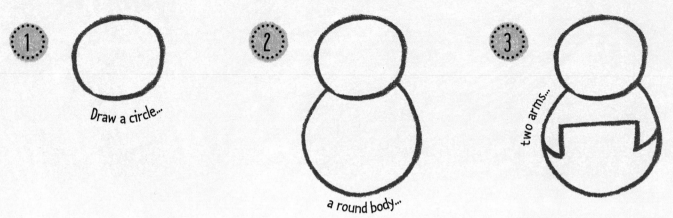

1. Draw a circle...

2. a round body...

3. two arms...

Your turn...

4 — two legs...

5 — two ears... a teardrop muzzle...

6 — eyes, a nose, a mouth... and a furry tummy.

Try this...

Follow the steps on the previous two pages to draw a bear on all fours. When you get to step 4, don't draw the panda eyes, but draw these instead...

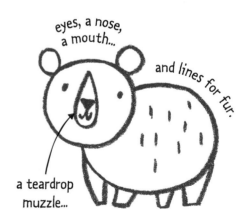

eyes, a nose, a mouth...

and lines for fur.

a teardrop muzzle...

How to draw a tourist

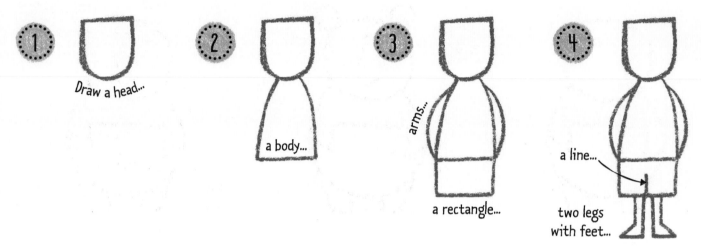

1 Draw a head...

2 a body...

3 arms... a rectangle...

4 a line... two legs with feet...

Your turn...

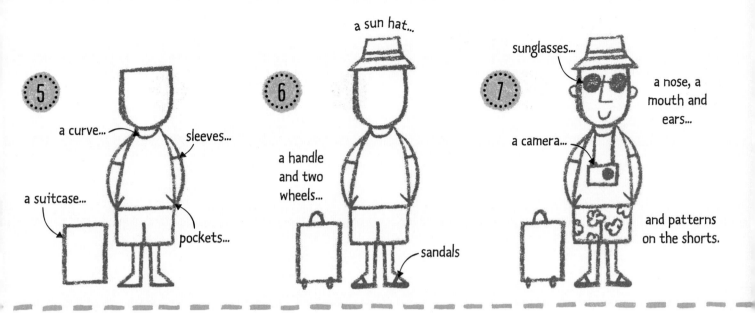

5 a curve... sleeves... a suitcase... pockets...

6 a sun hat... a handle and two wheels... sandals

7 sunglasses... a nose, a mouth and ears... a camera... and patterns on the shorts.

Draw more tourists and lots of suitcases.

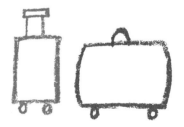

How to draw a spider

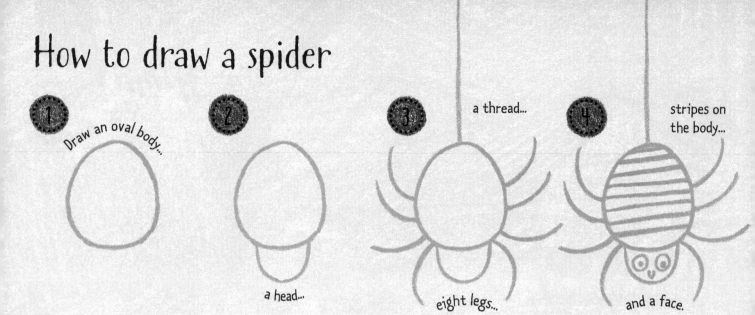

1. Draw an oval body...

2. a head...

3. a thread... eight legs...

4. stripes on the body... and a face.

Your turn...

...and a web.

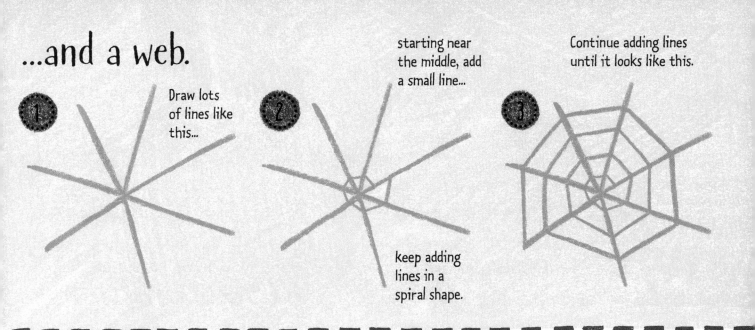

1 Draw lots of lines like this...

2 starting near the middle, add a small line...

keep adding lines in a spiral shape.

3 Continue adding lines until it looks like this.

How to draw a whale

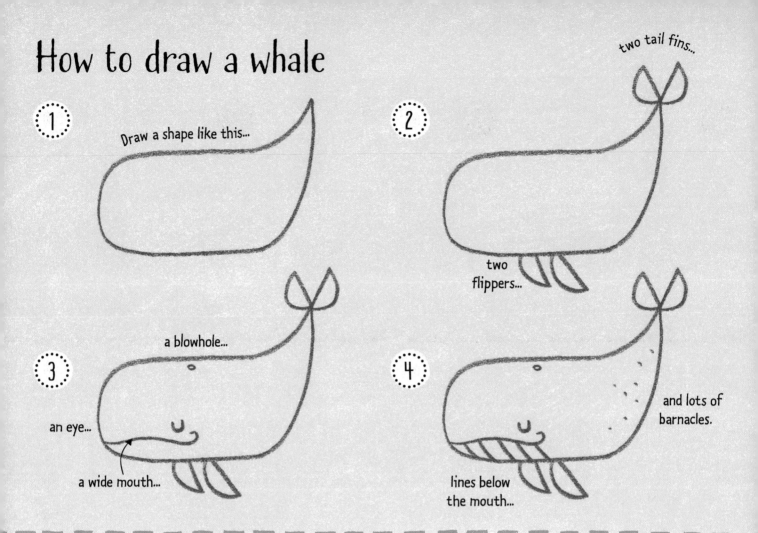

1 Draw a shape like this...

2 two tail fins...

two flippers...

3 a blowhole...

an eye...

a wide mouth...

4 and lots of barnacles.

lines below the mouth...

Your turn...

How to draw a monster

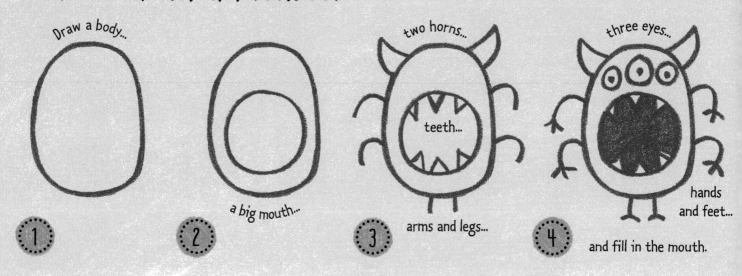

Draw a body...

a big mouth...

two horns...

teeth...

arms and legs...

three eyes...

hands and feet...

and fill in the mouth.

1   2   3   4

Your turn...

44

How to draw a firefighter

1 Draw a body...

like this...

2 a head...

a line...

3 an arm...

a nose...

4 two short lines...

a strap...

a glove...

a line...

Your turn...

5   a helmet...

a nozzle...

two legs...

6   a hose...

another arm and glove...

two boots...

7   an eye, a mouth and an ear...

a spray of water...

and reflective stripes.

How to draw a llama

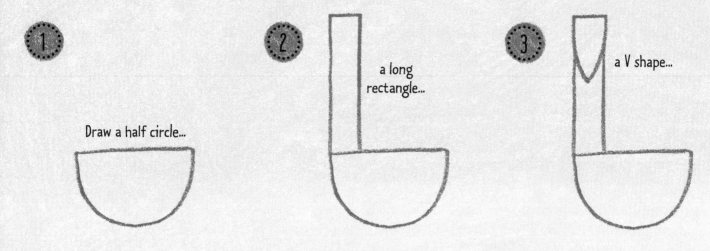

1 Draw a half circle...

2 a long rectangle...

3 a V shape...

Your turn...

48

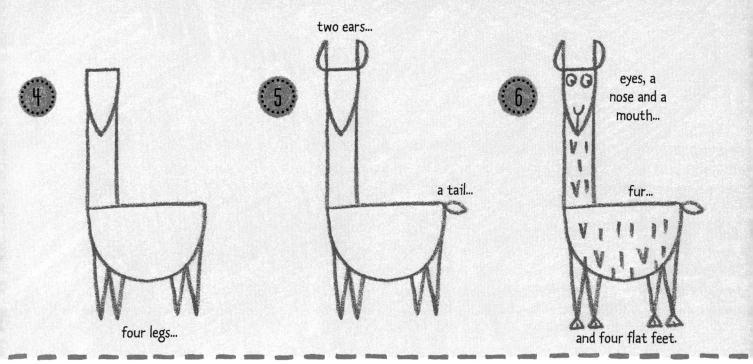

4 four legs...

5 two ears...
a tail...

6 eyes, a nose and a mouth...
fur...
and four flat feet.

How to draw a lizard

Your turn...

1

Draw a head...

2

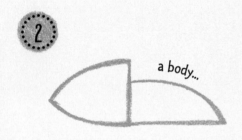

a body...

3

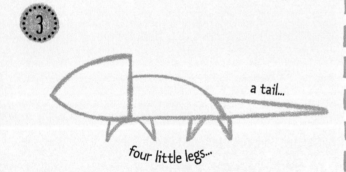

a tail...

four little legs...

4

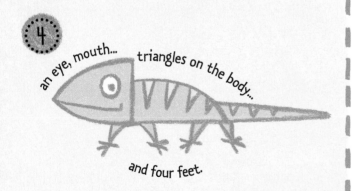

an eye, mouth....   triangles on the body...

and four feet.

How to draw a spy

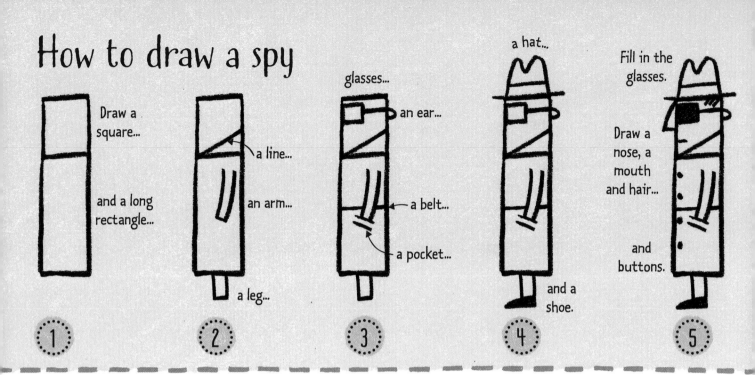

Draw a square...

and a long rectangle...

1

a line...

an arm...

a leg...

2

glasses...

an ear...

a belt...

a pocket...

3

a hat...

and a shoe.

4

Fill in the glasses.

Draw a nose, a mouth and hair...

and buttons.

5

Your turn...

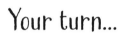

E Ploys only

This spy is handing over his secret briefcase. Draw more spies and briefcases in a park.

How to draw a camel

Draw a shape like
this...

1

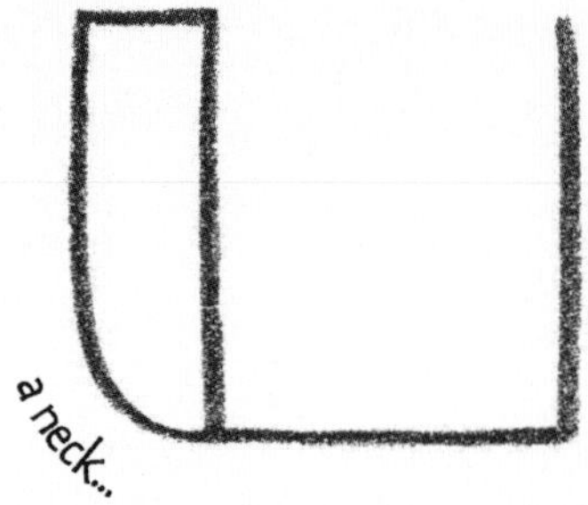

a neck...

2

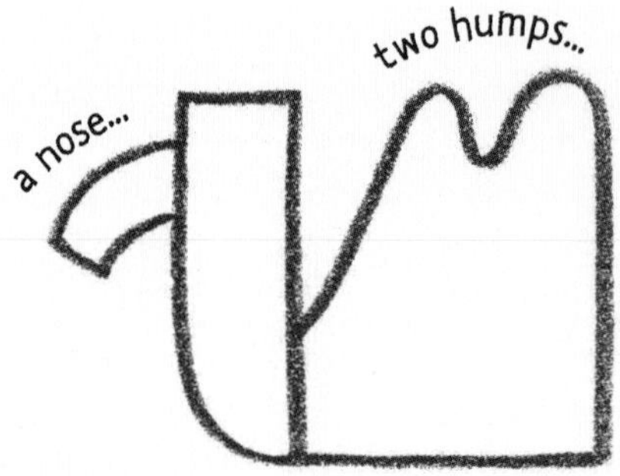

a nose...

two humps...

3

Your turn...

54

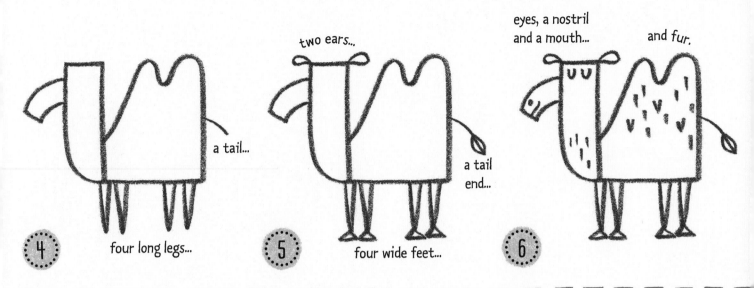

two ears...

eyes, a nostril and a mouth...

and fur.

a tail...

a tail end...

4 four long legs...

5 four wide feet...

6

Try this...

Some camels have only one hump. You could try copying the shape of this camel's body.

How to draw a penguin

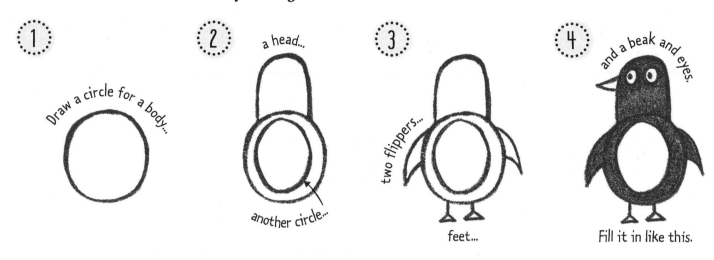

① Draw a circle for a body...

② a head...
another circle...

③ two flippers...
feet...

④ and a beak and eyes.
Fill it in like this.

Your turn...

How to draw a fox

Draw a rectangular body...

a head...

1

2

four legs...

3

Your turn...

a bushy tail...

4

two pointed ears...

a line on the chest...

5

zigzags on the tail...

a triangular stripe...

two eyes...

and a nose.

6

Try this...

To make your fox look like it's sitting down, draw the head, face and ears as above, then add...

a body like this and a bushy tail...

zigzags on the tail...

two front legs...

and one back leg.

How to draw faces

smiley surprised happy sad angry

tired excited upset asleep content

Your turn... Draw different expressions on these heads, then draw some of your own...

Add hair...

shaved   curly   straight   long   short   bunches

and accessories

glasses   eyebrows   beard   winter hat   cowboy hat   straw hat

How to draw a Roman

Your turn...

1 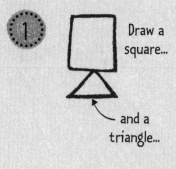 Draw a square...

and a triangle...

2 a tall rectangle...

3 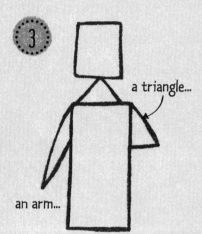 a triangle...

an arm...

4 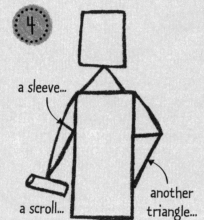 a sleeve...

a scroll...

another triangle...

5  hair...

hands...

legs and feet...

6 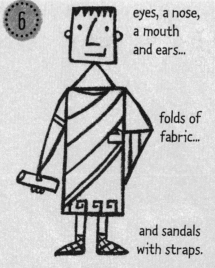 eyes, a nose, a mouth and ears...

folds of fabric...

and sandals with straps.

How to draw a horse

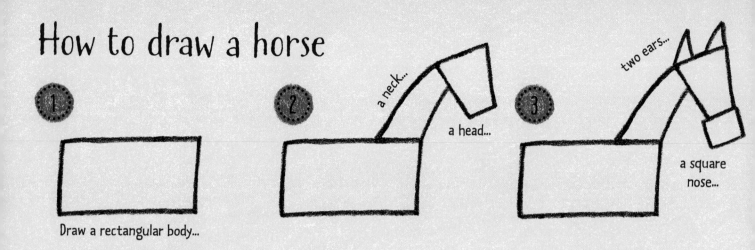

1 Draw a rectangular body...

2 a neck... a head...

3 two ears... a square nose...

Your turn...

4 four legs...

5 a tail...

a zigzag mane...

eyes...

and two nostrils.

You could draw shapes like these for grass.

How to draw a cowboy

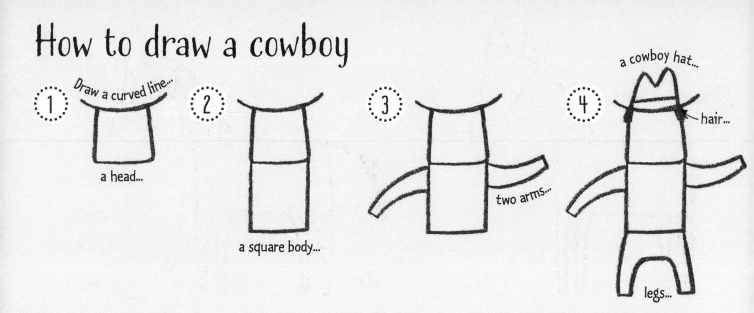

1. Draw a curved line...
   a head...

2. a square body...

3. two arms...

4. a cowboy hat...
   hair...
   legs...

Your turn...

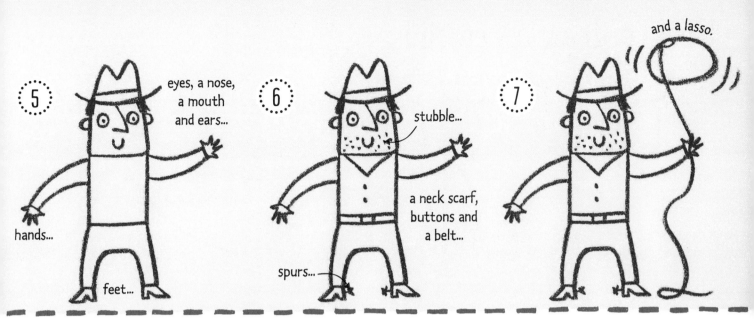

5 eyes, a nose, a mouth and ears...

hands...

feet...

6 stubble...

a neck scarf, buttons and a belt...

spurs...

7 and a lasso.

67

How to draw a cowgirl

Your turn...

1 Draw a curved line...

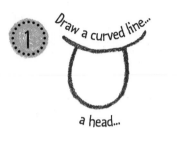

a head...

2

a body...

3

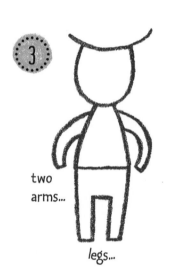

two arms...

legs...

4

a cowboy hat...

5

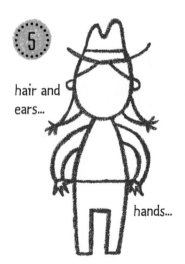

hair and ears...

hands...

6

her face...

a neck scarf...

belt and buttons...

and cowboy boots.

68

How to draw a puffin

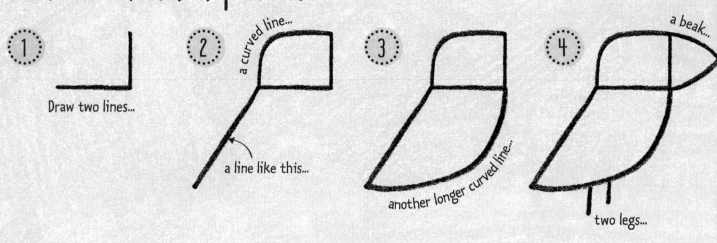

1 Draw two lines...

2 a curved line... a line like this...

3 another longer curved line...

4 a beak... two legs...

Your turn...

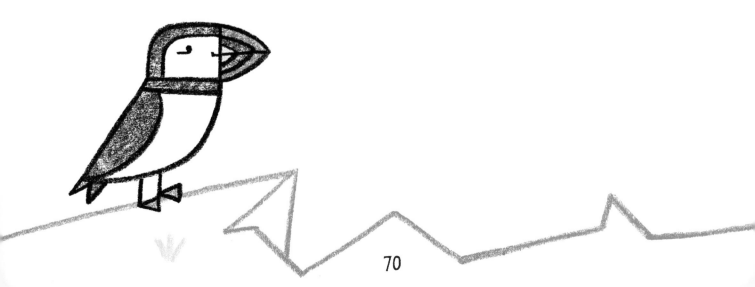

70

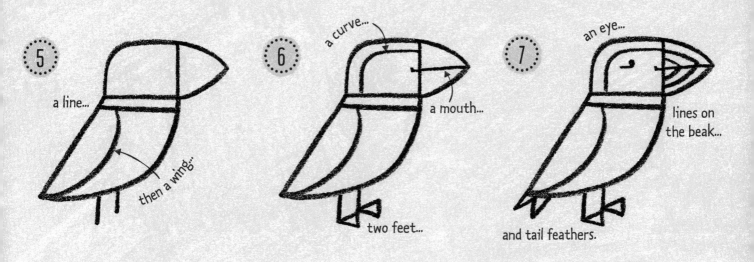

5

a line...

then a wing...

6

a curve...

a mouth...

two feet...

7

an eye...

lines on
the beak...

and tail feathers.

How to draw a lion

a curly mane...

Draw a head with ears...

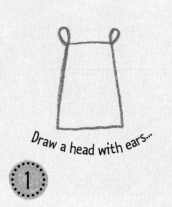

a body...

1   **2**   **3**

Your turn...

a nose, a mouth...

a tail...

the end of the tail...

teeth...

4

5

6

and add legs.

A lioness doesn't have a mane.

How to draw a singer

Your turn...

1 Draw a tilted square...

this shape for the body...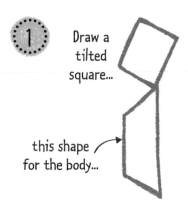

2 two short lines...

one longer line...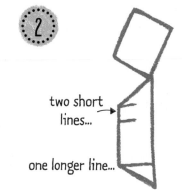

3 two arms...

4 a curve...

two legs...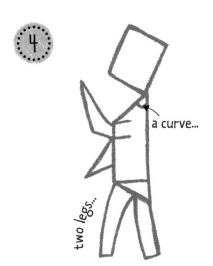

5 spiky hair...

a mouth...

hands...

feet...

6 a microphone...

stars...

and shoelaces.

eyes, a nose and ears...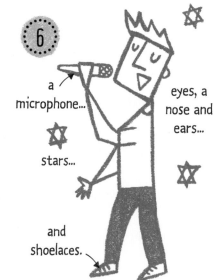

74

How to draw a movie star

Your turn...

1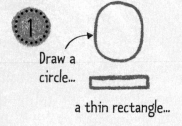
Draw a circle...

a thin rectangle...

2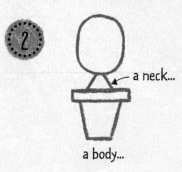
a neck...

a body...

3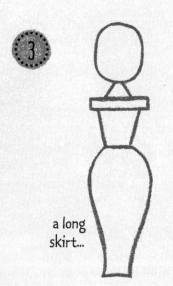
a long skirt...

4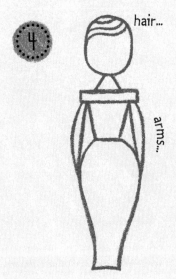
hair...

arms...

5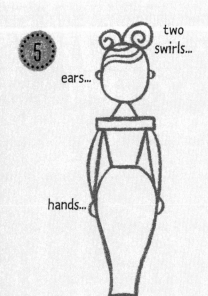
two swirls...

ears...

hands...

6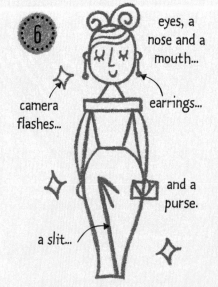
eyes, a nose and a mouth...

earrings...

camera flashes...

a slit...

and a purse.

How to draw a dog

Your turn...

 1

Draw a head...

an ear like a tear drop...

 2

a body...

 3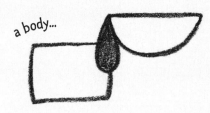

a tail...

four legs...

4

and an eye, mouth and nose.

You could add spots on the body.

Try this... use the same dog's head, but try different body shapes.

a hairy body   a long body   a square body   long legs

How to draw a seahorse

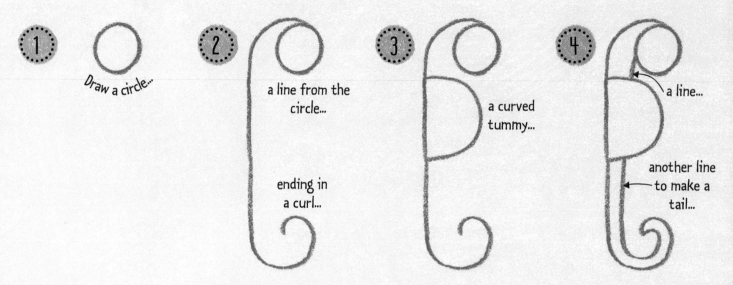

1 Draw a circle...

2 a line from the circle...

ending in a curl...

3 a curved tummy...

4 a line...

another line to make a tail...

Your turn...

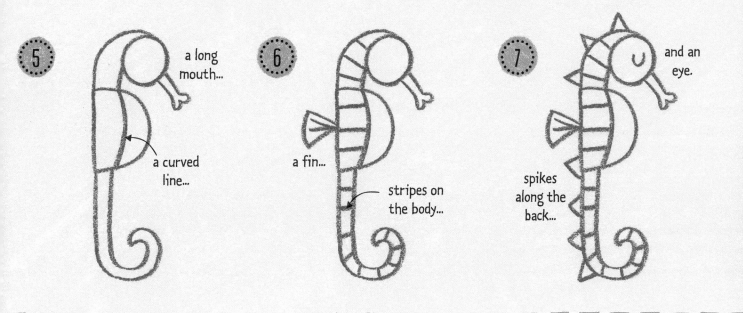

5 a long mouth...

a curved line...

6 a fin...

stripes on the body...

7 and an eye.

spikes along the back...

How to draw a hedgehog

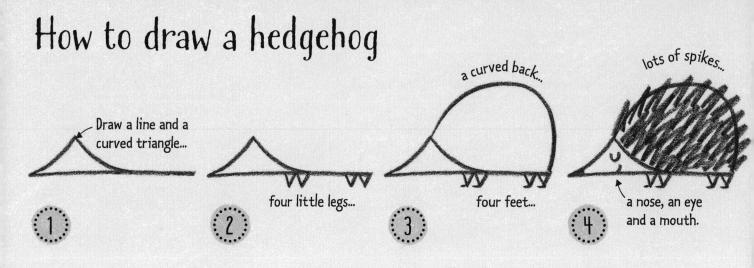

Draw a line and a curved triangle...

① four little legs...

② a curved back...

③ four feet...

④ lots of spikes...

a nose, an eye and a mouth.

Your turn...

How to draw a car

Your turn...

1

Draw a long rectangle...

2

a curved roof...

3

three windows...

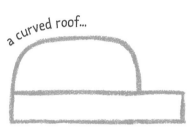

4

two wheels...

5

a rear
light...

front light...

and wheel arches.

Try different-shaped roofs.

How to draw a little boy

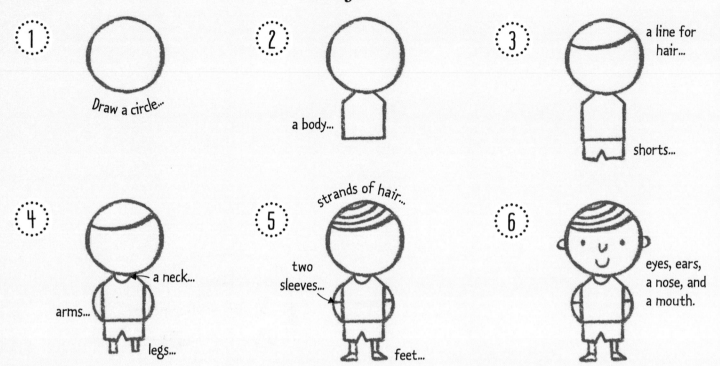

1. Draw a circle...

2. a body...

3. a line for hair... shorts...

4. a neck... arms... legs...

5. strands of hair... two sleeves... feet...

6. eyes, ears, a nose, and a mouth.

Your turn...

How to draw a little girl

① Draw a circle...

② a body...

③ a neck... a line for a skirt...

④ two curved lines... two arms... two legs...

⑤ pigtails... hands... feet...

⑥ eyes, ears, a nose, and a mouth... and pleats.

Your turn...

How to draw a goat

Your turn...

1 Draw a rectangle... and a small triangle...

2 a tail... a leaf-shaped head...

3 two teardrop ears... four legs...

4 two horns... fur... eyes, a nose and a mouth... and four hooves.

How to draw a shark

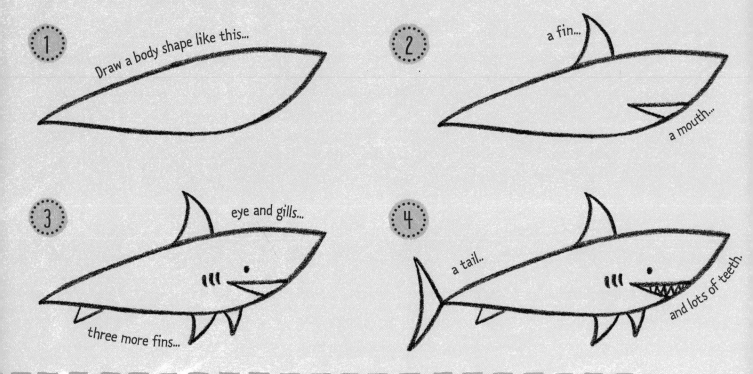

1 Draw a body shape like this...

2 a fin... a mouth...

3 eye and gills... three more fins...

4 a tail.. and lots of teeth.

Your turn...

How to draw a wolf

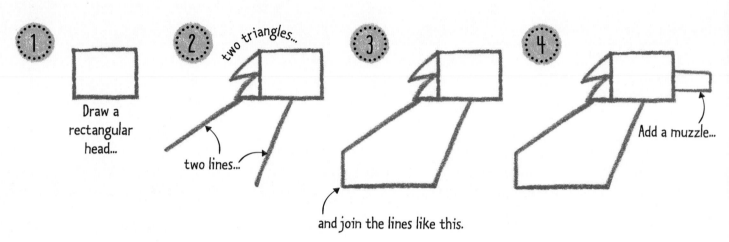

1 Draw a rectangular head...

2 two triangles... two lines...

3 and join the lines like this.

4 Add a muzzle...

Your turn...

Try drawing a howling wolf... just angle the head, open the mouth and add a closed eye.

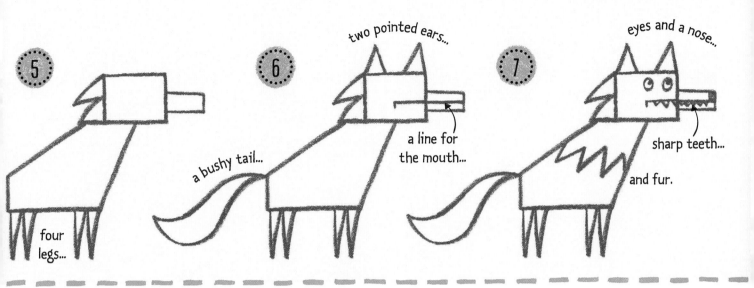

5 four legs...

6 two pointed ears...

a bushy tail...

a line for the mouth...

7 eyes and a nose...

sharp teeth...

and fur.

How to draw a mermaid

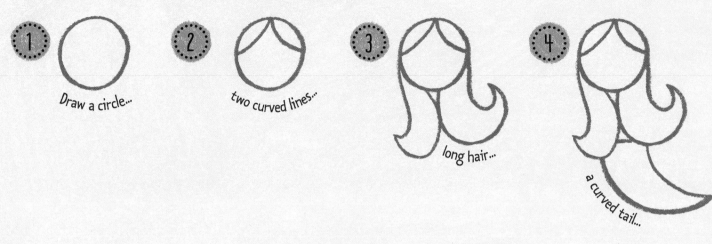

1 Draw a circle...

2 two curved lines...

3 long hair...

4 a curved tail...

Your turn...

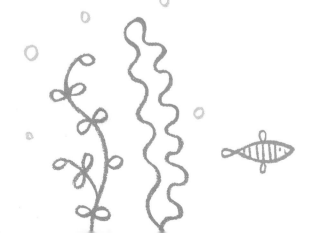

5 two arms...

6 lines in the hair... hands... two fins...

7 eyes, a nose, and a mouth. Add bubbles and fish... and scales.

How to draw an armadillo

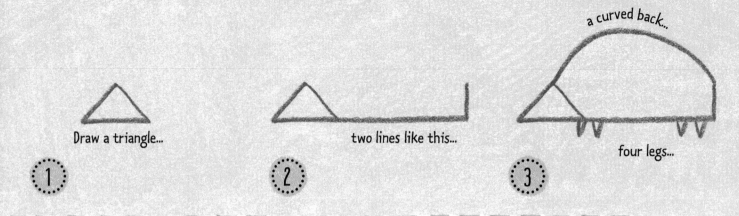

Draw a triangle...

①

two lines like this...

②

a curved back...

four legs...

③

Your turn...

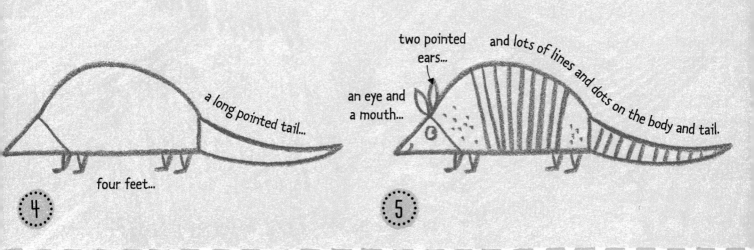

a long pointed tail...

four feet...

4

two pointed ears...

an eye and a mouth...

and lots of lines and dots on the body and tail.

5

99

How to draw a queen

1 Draw a head...

2 a body...

3 a curve... two arms...

4 a crown... ears... a big skirt...

Your turn...

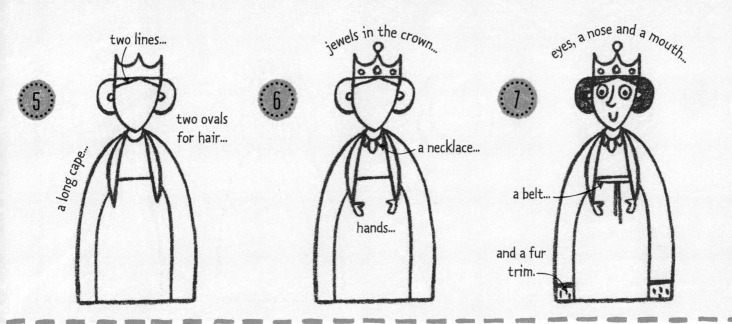

5 two lines...

a long cape...

two ovals for hair...

6 jewels in the crown...

a necklace...

hands...

7 eyes, a nose and a mouth...

a belt...

and a fur trim.

How to draw a king

1 Draw a head...

2 a big beard...

3 a body...

4 a crown...

Your turn...

5 ears...

sleeves...

two lines...

6 jewels in the crown...

hands...

a shirt...

a belt...

7 eyes, a nose and a mouth...

a staff...

and a fur trim.

How to draw an elephant

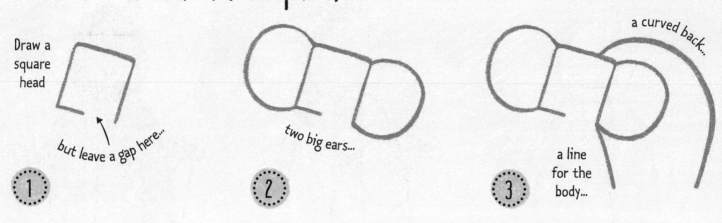

Draw a
square
head

but leave a gap here...

1

two big ears...

2

a curved back...

a line
for the
body...

3

- -

Your turn...

You could try drawing the trunk like this.

4 four legs...

5 a trunk...

6 a face, mouth... and a tail.
Add lines on the trunk, too.

How to draw a dragon

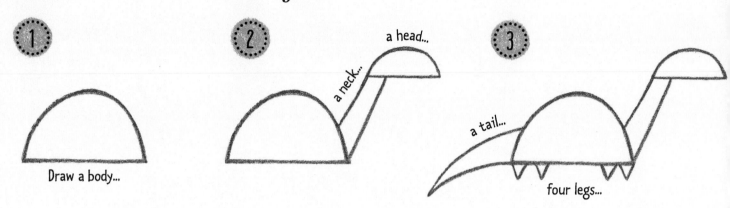

1 Draw a body...

2 a neck... a head...

3 a tail... four legs...

Your turn...

4 spikes...

four feet...

5 wings...

a face...

and flames.

How to draw a walrus

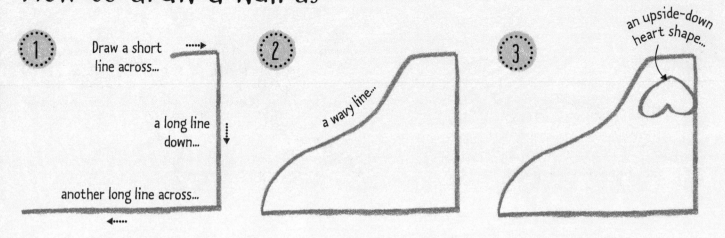

1 Draw a short line across...

a long line down...

another long line across...

2 a wavy line...

3 an upside-down heart shape...

Your turn...

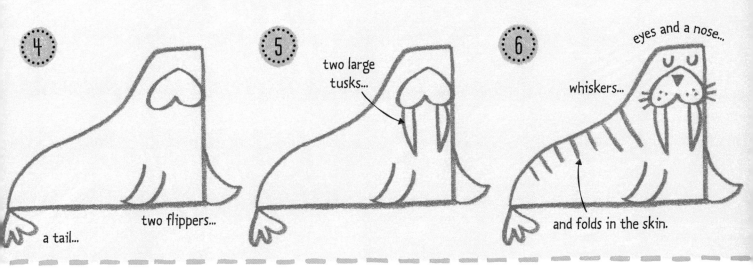

4 a tail...

two flippers...

5 two large tusks...

6 eyes and a nose...

whiskers...

and folds in the skin.

How to draw a princess

Your turn...

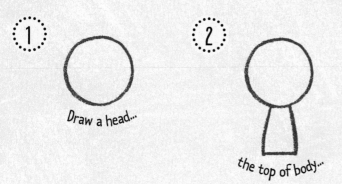

1 Draw a head...

2 the top of body...

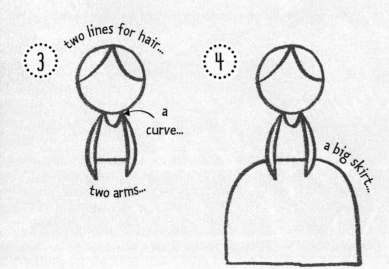

3 two lines for hair...
a curve...
two arms...

4 a big skirt...

5 a crown...
her face and ears...
long hair...

6 hands...
and patterns on the dress.

110

How to draw a badger

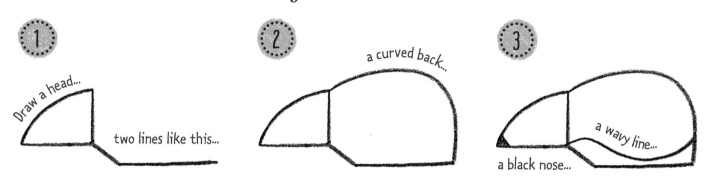

1 Draw a head... two lines like this...

2 a curved back...

3 a black nose... a wavy line...

Your turn...

4 a leaf shape... a tail...

four legs...

5 two ears... an eye and a mouth...

four feet...

6 and fur.

Fill in the shapes like this.

113

How to draw a monkey

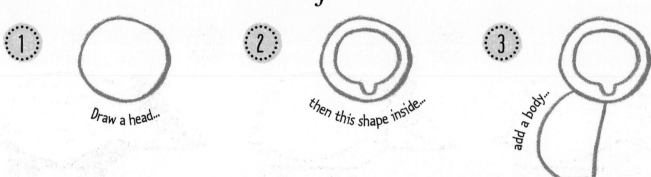

1 Draw a head...

2 then this shape inside...

3 add a body...

Your turn...

two ears...

④

a curly tail...

a back leg...

⑤

two front legs...

⑥

then add the face.

Try this...

Draw the same head that you drew before, then...

add two long arms...

a body...

a curly tail...

and two legs.

How to draw a mummy

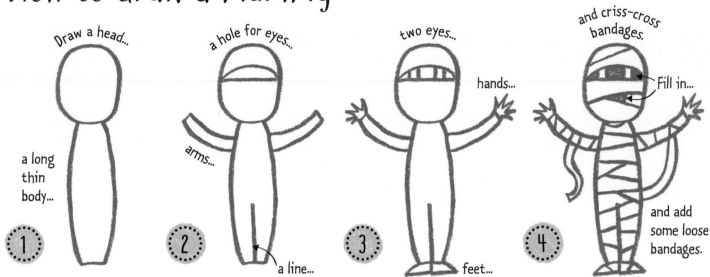

Draw a head...

a long thin body...

1

a hole for eyes...

arms...

a line...

2

two eyes...

hands...

feet...

3

and criss-cross bandages.

Fill in...

and add some loose bandages.

4

Your turn...

How to draw a castle

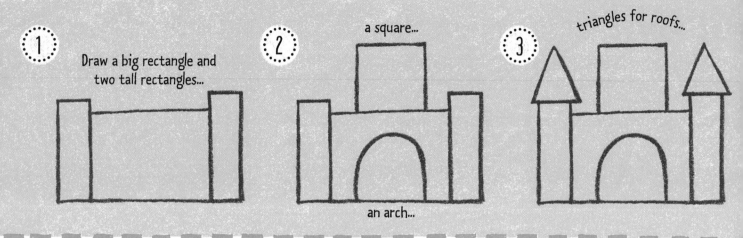

1 Draw a big rectangle and two tall rectangles...

2 a square...

an arch...

3 triangles for roofs...

Your turn...

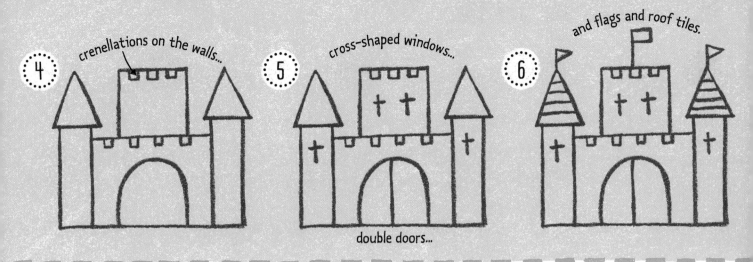

4 crenellations on the walls...

5 cross-shaped windows...

double doors...

6 and flags and roof tiles.

How to draw a knight

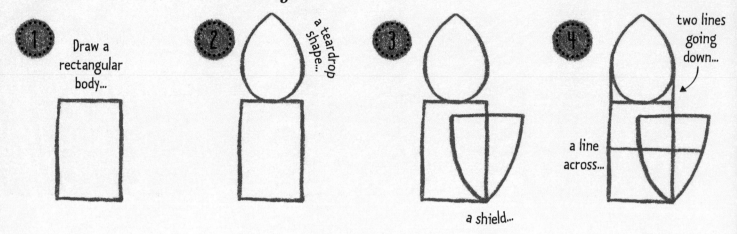

1 Draw a rectangular body...

2 a teardrop shape...

3 a shield...

4 two lines going down...

a line across...

Your turn...

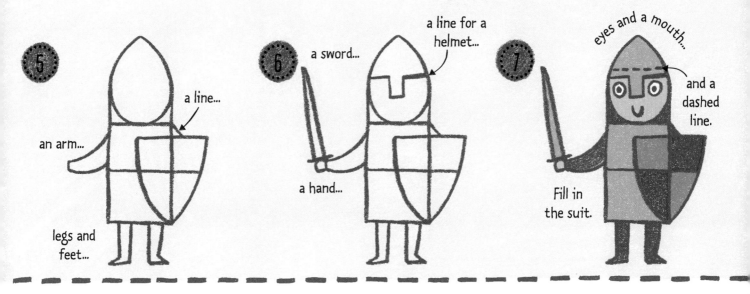

5 an arm...

a line...

legs and feet...

6 a sword...

a line for a helmet...

a hand...

7 eyes and a mouth...

and a dashed line.

Fill in the suit.

Try this...

Make your knight look different by...

using stripes instead of shading

drawing a full-face helmet

changing the shape of the shield

How to draw a snail

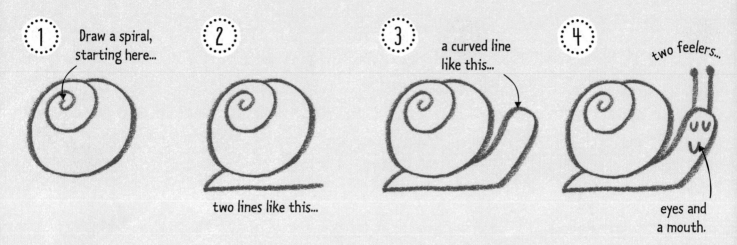

1. Draw a spiral, starting here...

2. two lines like this...

3. a curved line like this...

4. two feelers... eyes and a mouth.

Your turn...

Try this... vary the shape of the spiral and decorate to make different shells for your snail. How about...

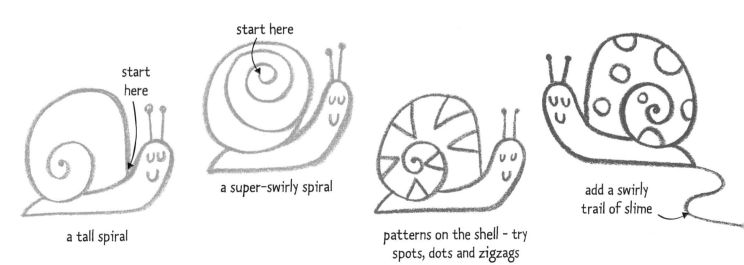

start
here

a tall spiral

start here

a super-swirly spiral

patterns on the shell - try
spots, dots and zigzags

add a swirly
trail of slime

How to draw a snake

Your turn...

1
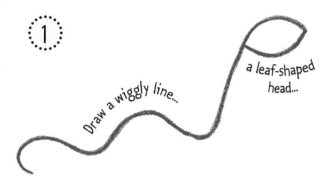
Draw a wiggly line...
a leaf-shaped head...

2
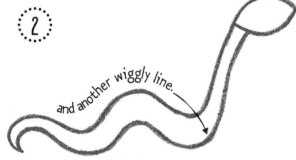
and another wiggly line.
Make the body fatter in the middle.

3
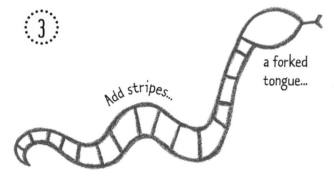
Add stripes...
a forked tongue...

4
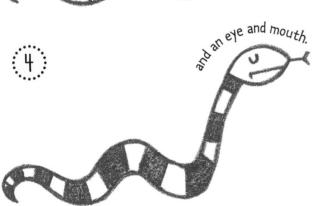
and an eye and mouth.
Fill in alternate squares.

How to draw a kokeshi doll

Draw a circle...

a body...

two sleeves...

a bun...

hair...

and a hand.

Fill in the hair...

draw a face and ears...

a kimono...

and two feet.

① ② ③ ④ ⑤

Your turn...

How to draw a rabbit

1 Draw a head...

2 two big ears...

3 a body...

Your turn...

4 a leg...
and a foot...

5 two front paws...

6 a face, whiskers...
and a tail.

Try this...

Draw the same rabbit head
that you drew before, then...

draw a body...

add a back leg and a tail...

and two front paws.

How to draw a turtle

Your turn...

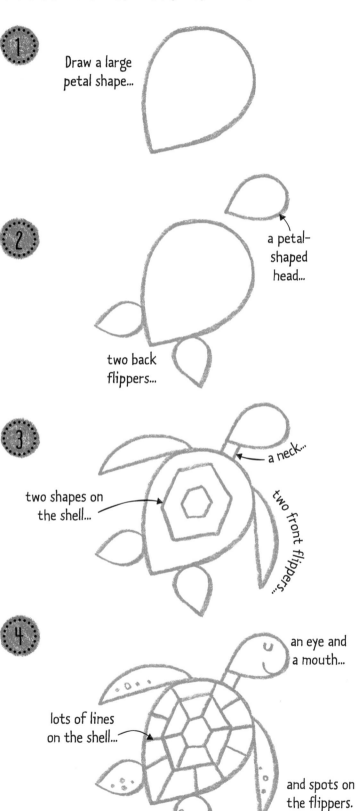

1 Draw a large petal shape...

2 a petal-shaped head...

two back flippers...

3 a neck...

two shapes on the shell...

two front flippers...

4 an eye and a mouth...

lots of lines on the shell...

and spots on the flippers.

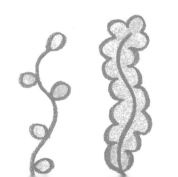

How to draw animal heads

koala squirrel seal puppy chicken pig

Your turn... Draw circles and then copy some of these simple faces...

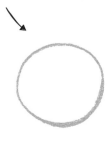

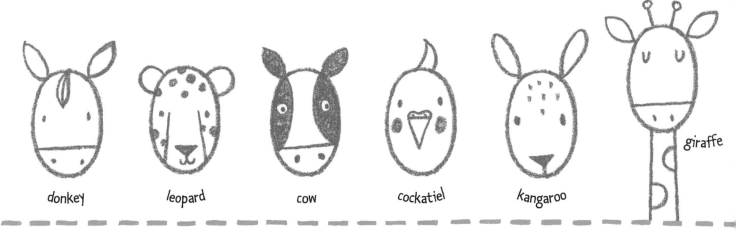

donkey leopard cow cockatiel kangaroo giraffe

Your turn... Draw ovals and then try these faces...

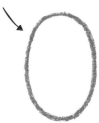

fox   raccoon   deer   dog   bison

snake   cat   goat   walrus   rhino

Your turn... Draw faces on these shapes, then try some more of your own...

How to draw a crab

Your turn...

1 Draw an oval...

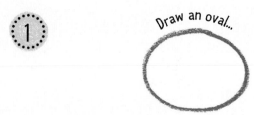

2 two lines...

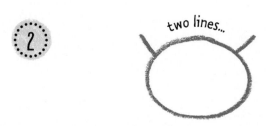

3 two large claws...

4 two lines...

four little legs on each side...

5 two eyes...

and a mouth.

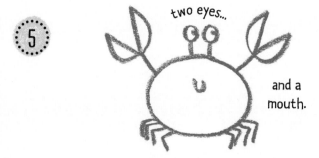

Try this... change the shape of the crab's body and alter the position of the claws.

claws in different positions   a leaf-shaped body and short claws   a rectangular body and long claws

How to draw a basketball player

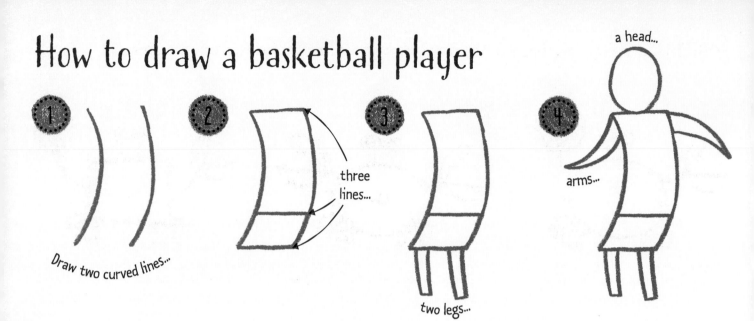

1 Draw two curved lines...

2 three lines...

3 two legs...

4 a head... arms...

Your turn...

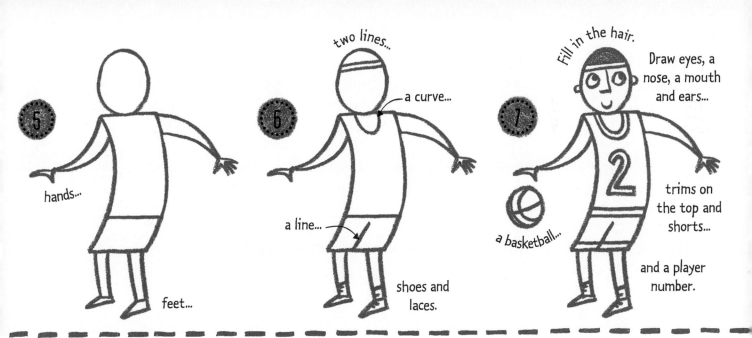

5 hands... feet...

6 two lines... a curve... a line... shoes and laces.

7 Fill in the hair. Draw eyes, a nose, a mouth and ears... trims on the top and shorts... and a player number. a basketball...

Try this...

Change the position of the legs to make your player run. Add some movement lines beneath the ball.

How to draw an alien

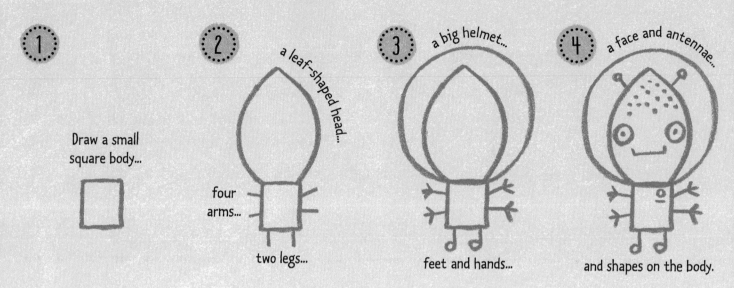

1 Draw a small square body...

2 a leaf-shaped head...

four arms...

two legs...

3 a big helmet...

feet and hands...

4 a face and antennae...

and shapes on the body.

Your turn...

Try an alien in a
spaceship. It doesn't
need a helmet.

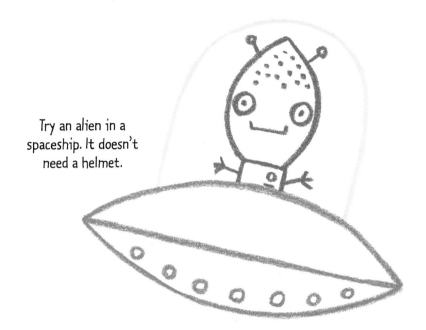

How to draw a Viking

1 Draw a rectangle...

2 a circle... and a smaller circle inside...

3 shoulders... a body...

4 a helmet... an arm... a rectangle...

Your turn...

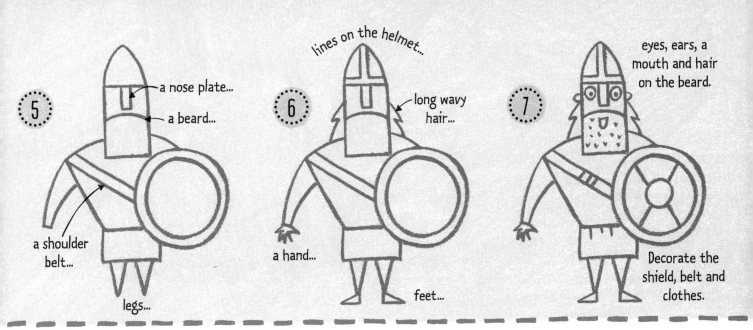

5 a nose plate...

a beard...

a shoulder belt...

legs...

6 lines on the helmet...

long wavy hair...

a hand...

feet...

7 eyes, ears, a mouth and hair on the beard.

Decorate the shield, belt and clothes.

How to draw a bird

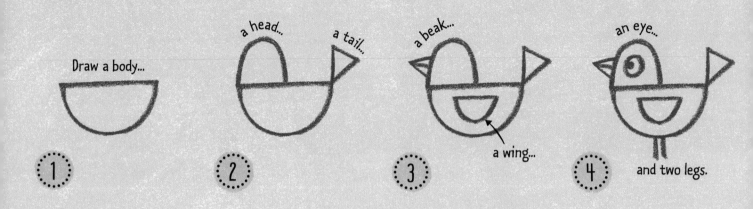

Draw a body...   a head...   a tail...   a beak...   a wing...   an eye...   and two legs.

① ② ③ ④

Your turn...

Try drawing different tails,
beaks, eyes and wings.

How to draw a chameleon

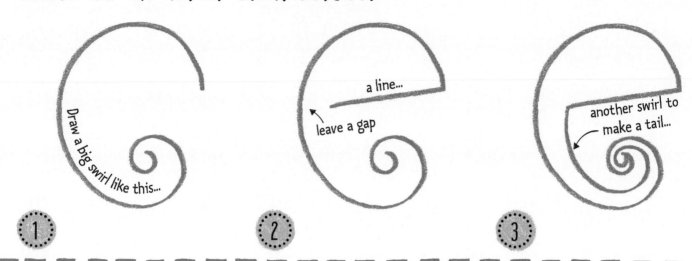

Draw a big swirl like this...

a line...

leave a gap

another swirl to make a tail...

1

2

3

Your turn...

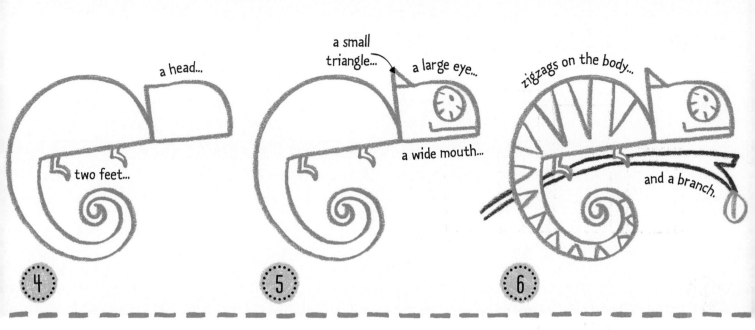

a head...

two feet...

4

a small triangle...

a large eye...

a wide mouth...

5

zigzags on the body...

and a branch.

6

How to draw a city

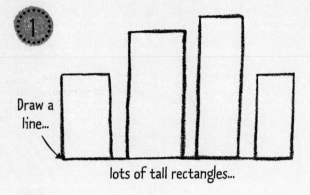

1

Draw a
line...

lots of tall rectangles...

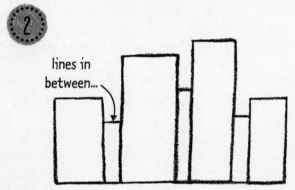

2

lines in
between...

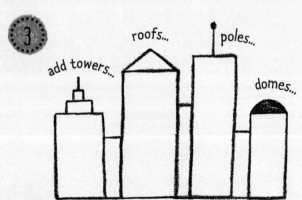

3

add towers...

roofs...

poles...

domes...

4

and lots
of windows.

How to draw a witch

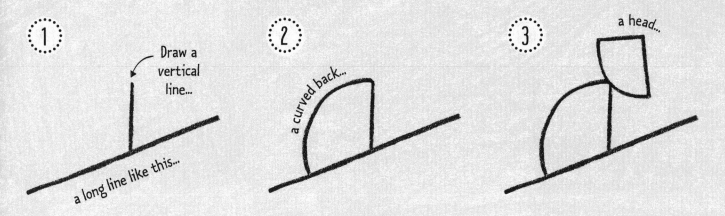

1 Draw a vertical line...

a long line like this...

2 a curved back...

3 a head...

Your turn...

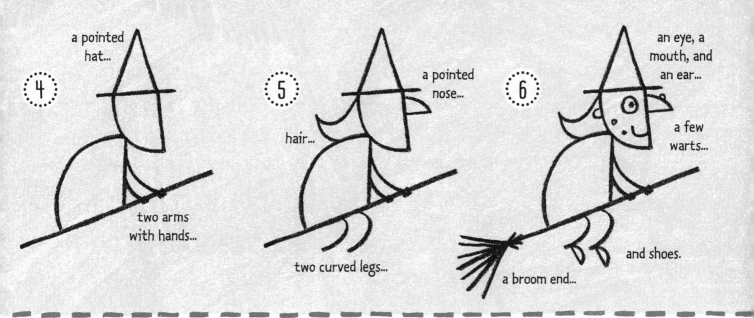

4 a pointed hat...

two arms with hands...

5 a pointed nose...

hair...

two curved legs...

6 an eye, a mouth, and an ear...

a few warts...

a broom end...

and shoes.

Try this...

To draw a spooky witch silhouette, first draw a large yellow circle for the moon, then follow the steps above. Instead of adding a face, fill in the whole shape so that it looks like this:

How to draw a kangaroo

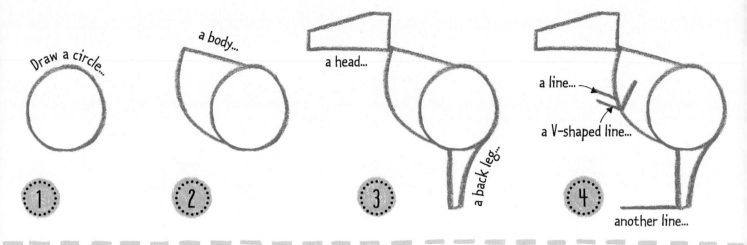

Draw a circle...

1

a body...

2

a head...

a back leg...

3

a line...

a V-shaped line...

another line...

4

Your turn...

5 a hand... the top of the foot... a thick tail...

6 two ears... an eye, a nose and a mouth... and fur.

Try this...

Draw a jumping kangaroo by changing the position of the back leg. You could also add a baby joey in a pouch.

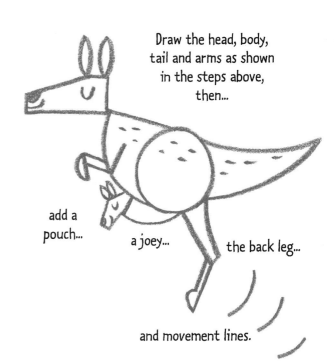

Draw the head, body, tail and arms as shown in the steps above, then...

add a pouch...

a joey...

the back leg...

and movement lines.

How to draw an astronaut

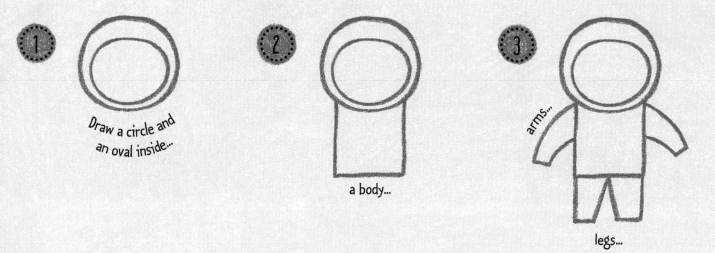

1 Draw a circle and an oval inside...

2 a body...

3 arms... legs...

Your turn...

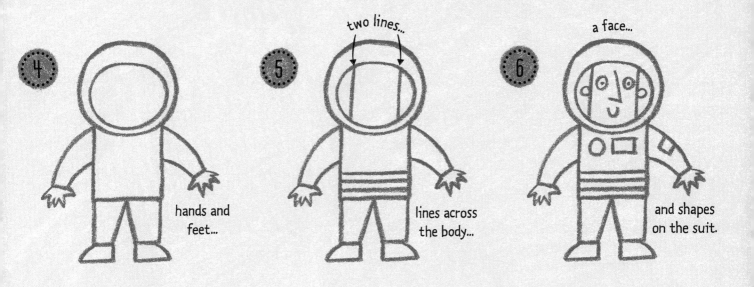

4 hands and feet...

5 two lines... lines across the body...

6 a face... and shapes on the suit.

How to draw a giraffe

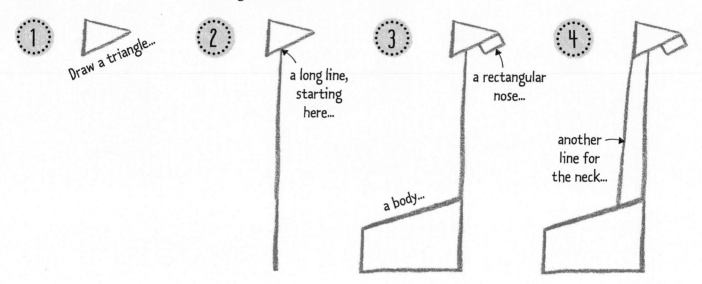

1 Draw a triangle...

2 a long line, starting here...

3 a body... a rectangular nose...

4 another line for the neck...

Your turn...

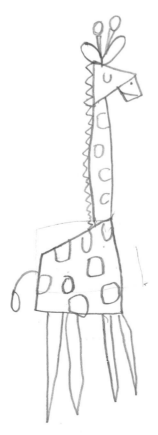

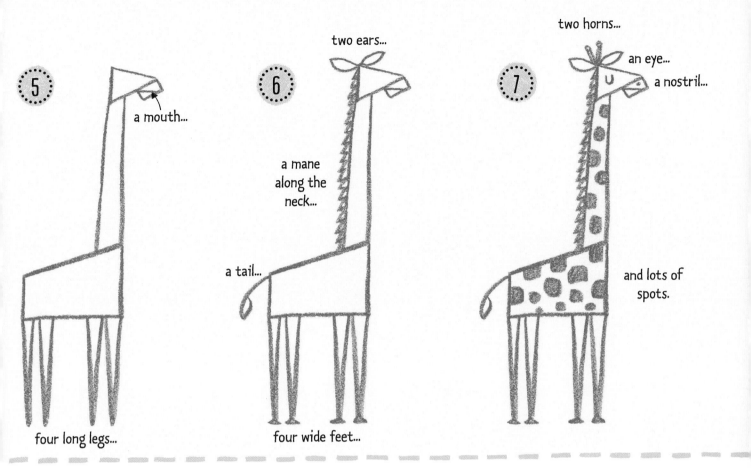

5 a mouth...

four long legs...

6 two ears...

a mane along the neck...

a tail...

four wide feet...

7 two horns...

an eye...

a nostril...

and lots of spots.

How to draw a doctor

Your turn...

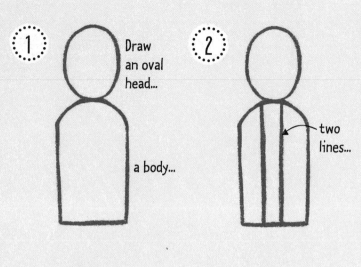

1 Draw an oval head...

a body...

2 two lines...

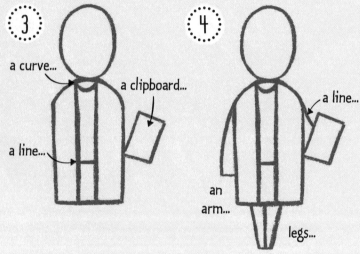

3 a curve...

a clipboard...

a line...

4 a line...

an arm...

legs...

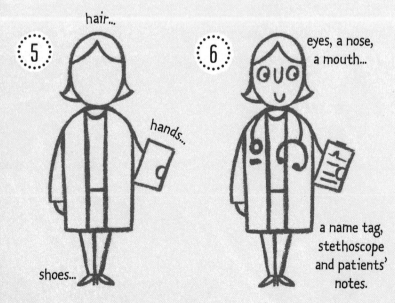

5 hair...

hands...

shoes...

6 eyes, a nose, a mouth...

a name tag, stethoscope and patients' notes.

156

How to draw a nurse

Your turn...
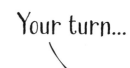

1 Draw a square head...

a body...

2 legs...

3 a V shape...

a line for the legs...

4 two small triangles...

a folder...

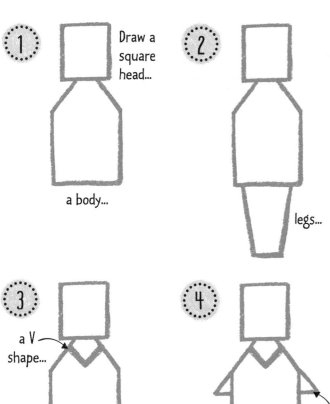

5 hair...

two arms...

a hand...

shoes...

6 eyes, a nose, a mouth and ears...

a name tag and a watch.

How to draw bugs

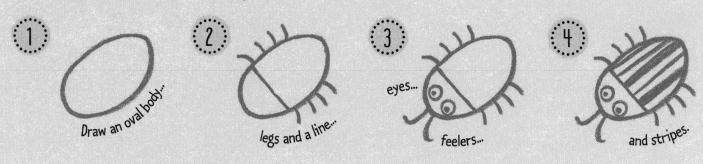

① Draw an oval body...

② legs and a line...

③ eyes... feelers...

④ and stripes.

Your turn...

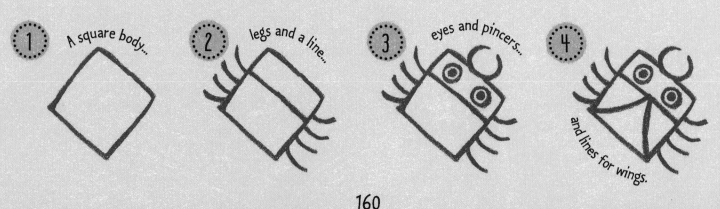

① A square body...

② legs and a line...

③ eyes and pincers...

④ and lines for wings.

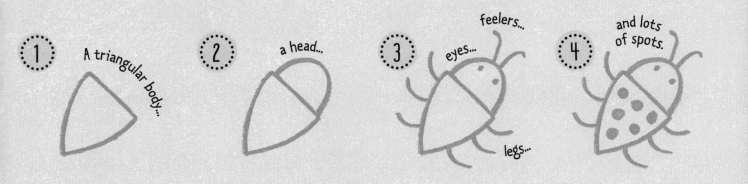

1 A triangular body...

2 a head...

3 feelers... eyes... legs...

4 and lots of spots.

1 A round body...

2 a head...

3 feelers... eyes... legs...

4 and zigzag lines.

161

How to draw a polar bear

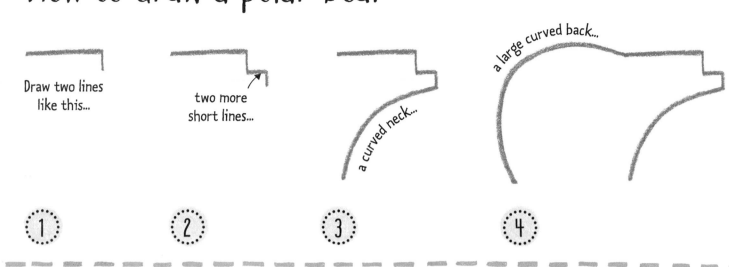

Draw two lines
like this...

two more
short lines...

a curved neck...

a large curved back...

① ② ③ ④

Your turn...

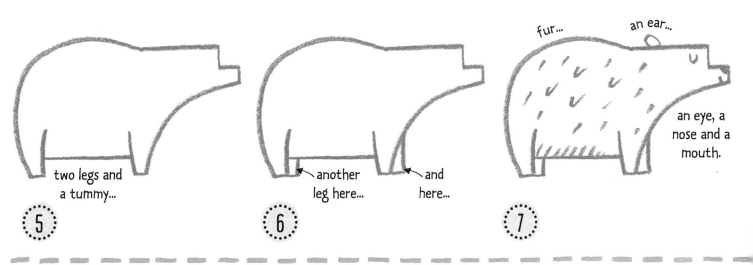

two legs and
a tummy...

another
leg here...

and
here...

fur...

an ear...

an eye, a
nose and a
mouth.

5

6

7

How to draw a koala

Your turn...

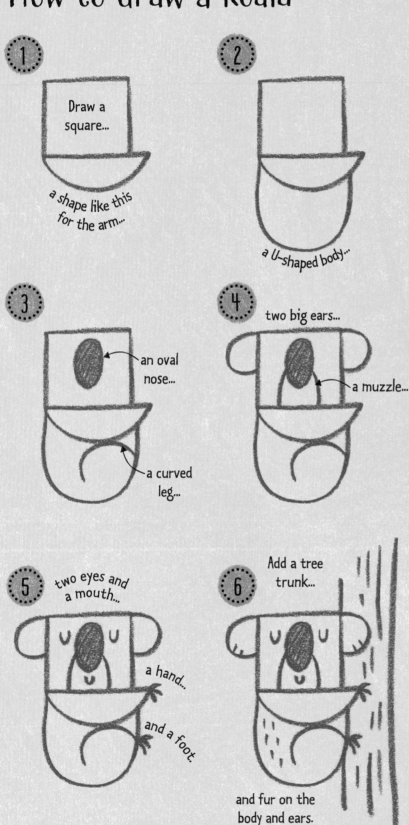

1 Draw a square...

a shape like this for the arm...

2 a U-shaped body...

3 an oval nose...

a curved leg...

4 two big ears...

a muzzle...

5 two eyes and a mouth...

a hand...

and a foot.

6 Add a tree trunk...

and fur on the body and ears.

How to draw a pirate ship

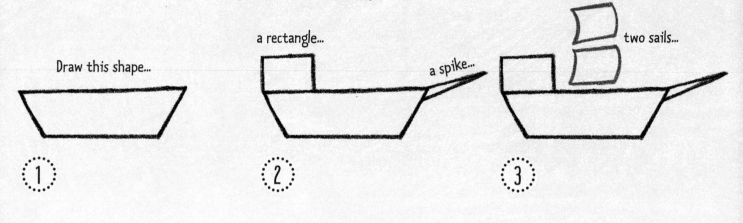

Draw this shape...

a rectangle...

a spike...

two sails...

①

②

③

Your turn...

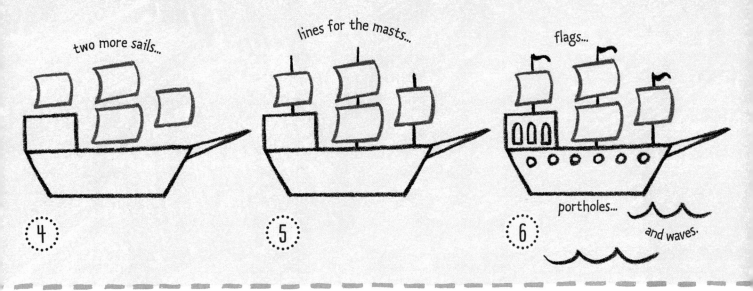

two more sails...

lines for the masts...

flags...

portholes...

and waves.

④

⑤

⑥

167

How to draw a pirate

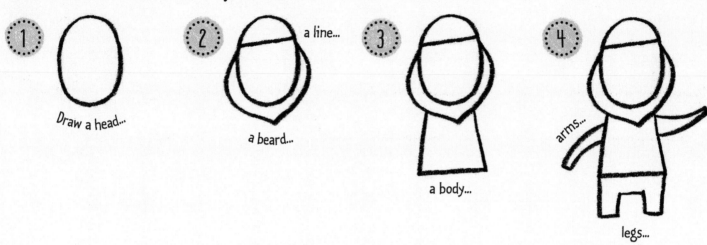

1 Draw a head...

2 a beard... a line...

3 a body...

4 arms... legs...

Your turn...

168

5   ears... hands... feet...

6   a bow... a cutlass... buttons, a belt and a buckle...

7   and a face with an eye patch.

How to draw a parrot

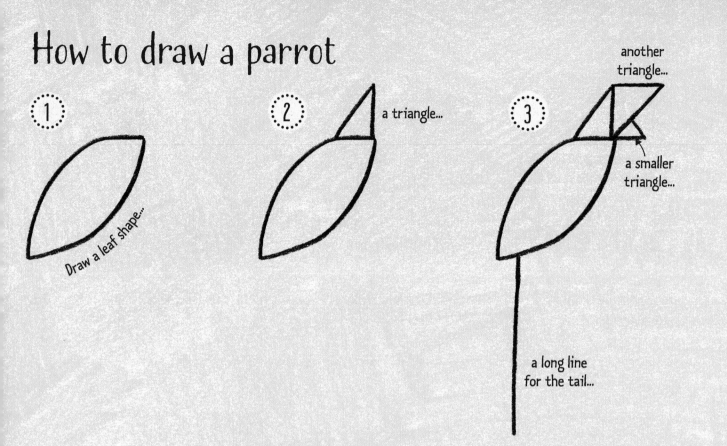

1 Draw a leaf shape...

2 a triangle...

3 another triangle...

a smaller triangle...

a long line for the tail...

Your turn...

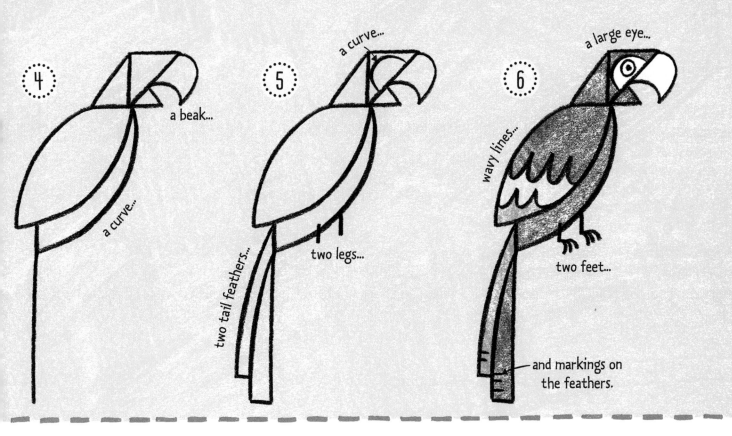

4 a beak... a curve...

5 a curve... two tail feathers... two legs...

6 a large eye... wavy lines... two feet... and markings on the feathers.

How to draw a pirate captain

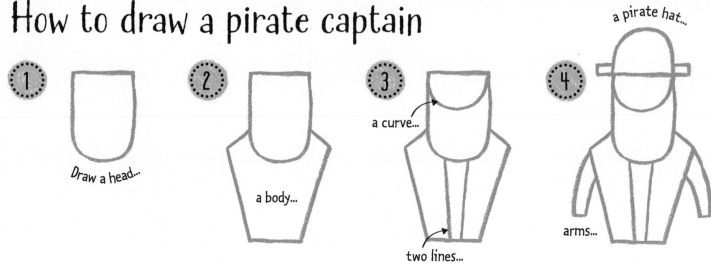

① Draw a head...

② a body...

③ a curve... two lines...

④ a pirate hat... arms...

Your turn...

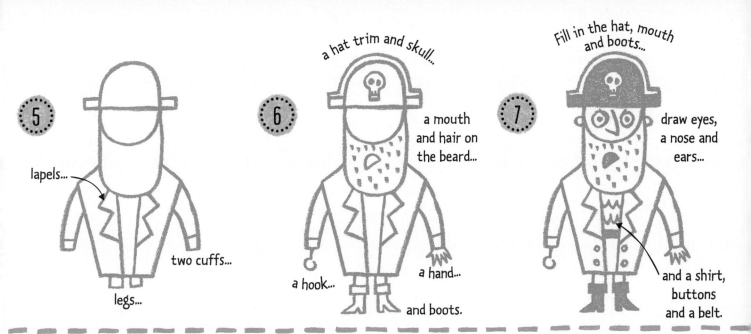

5 lapels... two cuffs... legs...

6 a hat trim and skull... a mouth and hair on the beard... a hook... a hand... and boots.

7 Fill in the hat, mouth and boots... draw eyes, a nose and ears... and a shirt, buttons and a belt.

173

How to draw a tiger

1 Draw a square head... and a body...

2 a long tail... two ears...

3 a face... two front legs...

4 and cover with stripes.

Your turn...

How to draw a chef

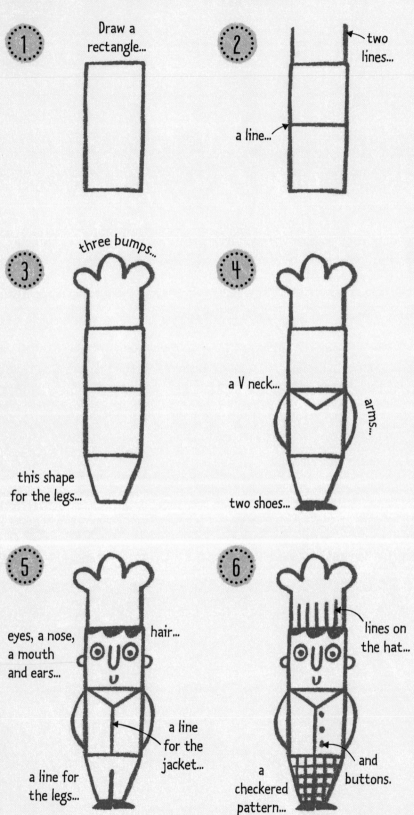

1 Draw a rectangle...

2 two lines...

a line...

3 three bumps...

this shape for the legs...

4 a V neck...

arms...

two shoes...

5 eyes, a nose, a mouth and ears...

hair...

a line for the jacket...

a line for the legs...

6 lines on the hat...

and buttons.

a checkered pattern...

How to draw an explorer

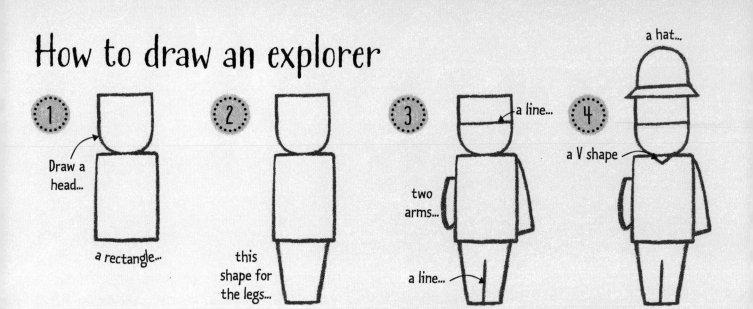

1 Draw a head...

a rectangle...

2 this shape for the legs...

3 a line...

two arms...

a line...

4 a hat...

a V shape

Your turn...

Draw large leaves around your explorer - he'll look like he's in the jungle.

178

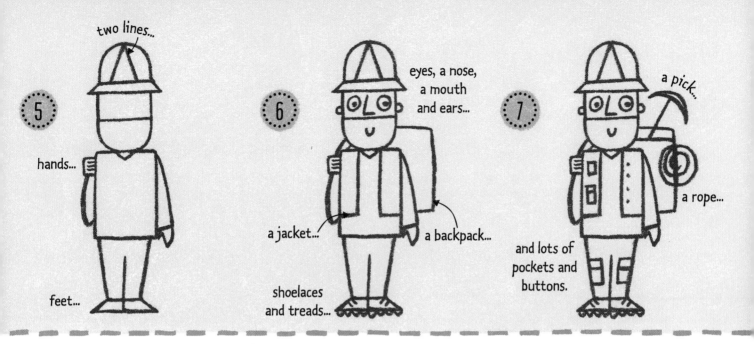

5

two lines...

hands...

feet...

6

eyes, a nose, a mouth and ears...

a jacket...

a backpack...

shoelaces and treads...

7

a pick...

a rope...

and lots of pockets and buttons.

Try this...

To draw an Arctic explorer, add boots, a warm jacket and a fur-lined hood instead.

fur hood

warm jacket

snow boots

How to draw a butterfly

Your turn...

1 Draw a long petal shape...

2 two large wings...

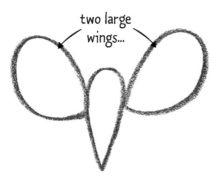

3 a face...

two smaller wings...

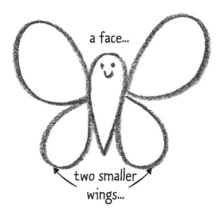

4 two feelers...

spots on the top wings...

and stripes on the body.

stripes on the bottom wings...

Try drawing some butterflies with different patterns on their wings.

How to draw a ballerina

1 Draw a circle...

2 a body...

3 hair... a skirt...

4 a bun... arms... legs...

5 two hands... a curve... two feet...

6 ears... eyes, a nose and a mouth... ruffles on the skirt... and ballet shoes with ribbons.

Your turn...

Try this...

Draw your ballerina in different positions by altering the legs, arms or both. Here are some ideas. You could copy these or try your own.

arms up

legs crossed

arms down

legs crossed, feet flat

arm down

arm up

balanced on one leg

How to draw a crocodile

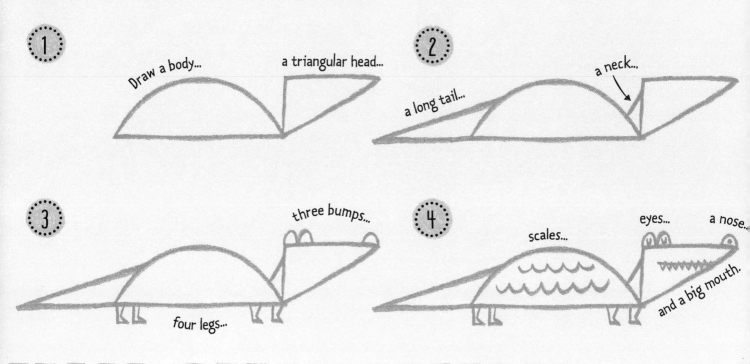

1 Draw a body... a triangular head...

2 a neck... a long tail...

3 three bumps... four legs...

4 scales... eyes... a nose... and a big mouth.

Your turn...

Try this...

For a crocodile swimming in water - don't bother to draw the feet. Just draw wavy lines for water.

How to draw an ice skater

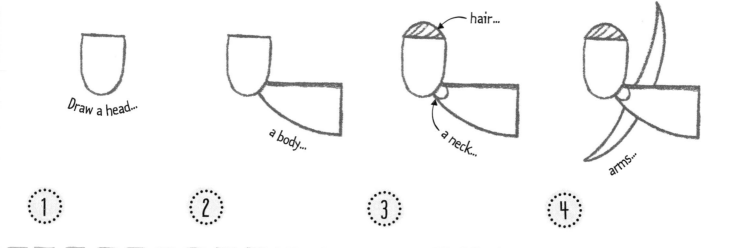

Draw a head...

①

a body...

②

hair...

a neck...

③

arms...

④

Your turn...

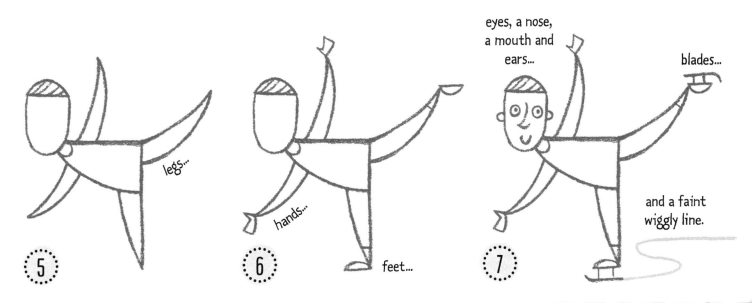

5 legs...

6 hands... feet...

7 eyes, a nose, a mouth and ears... blades... and a faint wiggly line.

How to draw a rhino

1 Draw this shape for the body...

2 a curved line... and another...

3 the back of the head... a mouth and a snout...

4 four legs...

5 two ears... two horns... a tail...

6 an eye and a nostril. folds in the skin...

Your turn...

How to draw a circus strongman

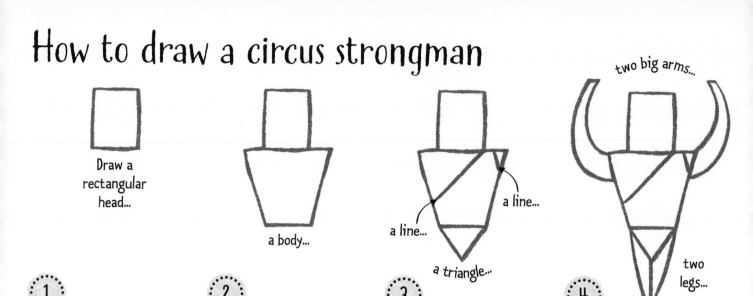

Draw a
rectangular
head...

a body...

a line...

a line...

a triangle...

two big arms...

two
legs...

1

2

3

4

Your turn...

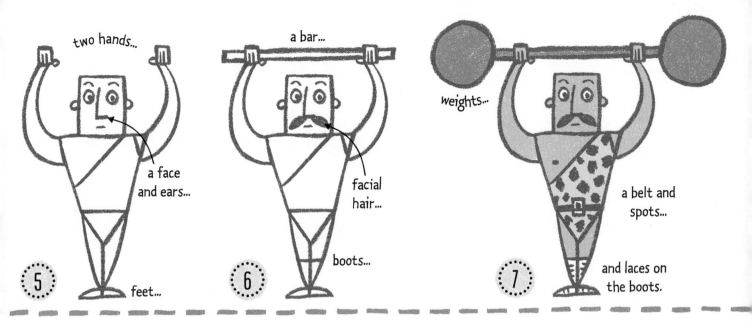

two hands...

a face
and ears...

5

feet...

a bar...

facial
hair...

6

boots...

weights...

a belt and
spots...

7

and laces on
the boots.

How to draw an owl

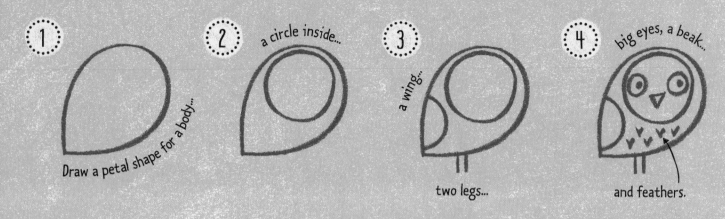

1. Draw a petal shape for a body...

2. a circle inside...

3. a wing... two legs...

4. big eyes, a beak... and feathers.

Your turn...

First published in 2015 by Usborne Publishing Ltd., Usborne House, 83-85 Saffron Hill, London EC1N 8RT, England.
www.usborne.com © 2015, 2014 Usborne Publishing Ltd. The name Usborne and the devices are Trade Marks of Usborne Publishing Ltd.